# If You Ain't Going To Lead

## Don't Spit

Humorous Motorcycle
and
Leadership Stories

### Col. Layton Park

# *If You Are Going To Lead...*
# *Don't Spit!*

An anthology of humour from Layton Park's columns:
*Park on the Boulevard*
*Smart Ass Jack*
*Back Road Scholar*
*Park on the Road*

*Preparing for his ride around America*

By Col. Layton Park

Edited by Jessi Hoffman
Sherilyn Williams

iUniverse, Inc.
Bloomington

# If You Are Going to Lead... Don't Spit!

Copyright © 2011 by Col. Layton Park

All rights reserved. No part of this book may be used or reproduced by any means, graphic, electronic, or mechanical, including photocopying, recording, taping or by any information storage retrieval system without the written permission of the publisher except in the case of brief quotations embodied in critical articles and reviews.

The information, ideas, and suggestions in this book are not intended to render professional advice. Before following any suggestions contained in this book, you should consult your personal accountant or other financial advisor. Neither the author nor the publisher shall be liable or responsible for any loss or damage allegedly arising as a consequence of your use or application of any information or suggestions in this book.

iUniverse books may be ordered through booksellers or by contacting:

iUniverse
1663 Liberty Drive
Bloomington, IN 47403
www.iuniverse.com
1-800-Authors (1-800-288-4677)

Because of the dynamic nature of the Internet, any web addresses or links contained in this book may have changed since publication and may no longer be valid. The views expressed in this work are solely those of the author and do not necessarily reflect the views of the publisher, and the publisher hereby disclaims any responsibility for them.

Any people depicted in stock imagery provided by Thinkstock are models, and such images are being used for illustrative purposes only.

Certain stock imagery © Thinkstock.

ISBN: 978-1-4620-1884-0 (sc)
ISBN: 978-1-4620-1885-7 (ebk)

Printed in the United States of America

iUniverse rev. date: 05/16/2011

# Col. Layton Park
### C.Ht. CPBA, CPVA, RET

Layton and his wife Myrna are engaged in business consulting especially with improving the people side of business. They have run Max-U inc since the late 1990's and say it is a GPS4Biz as they work with senior management to help companies establish exactly where they are, quantify where they want to be and then decide on the best course to take them there. Both, Layton and Myrna have spent years studying human behavior in business and sales working with a number of organizations, sports teams, and individual clients looking to make positive changes and improve mental toughness.

This work has taken Layton to all parts of the globe. In the former Soviet Union State of Kazakhstan, he acted as consultant to several companies in making the change to a western style of business.

Layton began his own design-build company in 1975 and grew it into a business with more than 80 direct employees and several contractors. He was also a partner in a successful real estate company, served as president of the local real estate board, sat on the advisory board to a Trust Company and served two terms as president of Canadian Authors Association, Kelowna Branch.

Layton has been a partner in several service-focused businesses and is an active partner in: Max-U. Inc., a provider of training and speaking programs, Parkline Services, a development company, LAMP Land Inc., a lighting and décor business and The Canadian Hypnosis Institute.

Layton has spoken on business topics across Canada, the U.S., Mexico, and Kazakhstan, has authored a number of books and pens monthly humor columns.

The honorary title of, Colonel, was conferred on Layton by Paul Patton, Governor of Kentucky.

An aviation enthusiast, he has flown his airplanes over 480,000 kilometers across the great Canadian north.

This book is a collection of humour columns printed in the motorcycle newspaper, the Busted Knuckle, and assembled to combine Layton's thoughts on leadership with his love for motorcycling.

Any biker will tell you that riding at the head of the dragon is not as easy as it seems as you have to always be thinking about those riding behind you. The metaphor, *"If You Are Going to Lead, Don't Spit"* is a tongue in cheek (if you pardon the pun) reference to the laws of aerodynamics, which say if you are the front biker and spit someone following you will wear it.

In business, if you spit or let other negative things leave your mouth you can be sure that if it does not fly back and hit you, it will strike one of your followers.

Mostly the stories are simply light humorous essays about life as a biker but reflecting on them one can see some of the characteristics of leadership. Please enjoy.

Layton is available for business consulting, as well as educational, inspirational, and humorous public presentations for more information contact: Info@max-u.com.

☙

*If you ride like there's no tomorrow, there won't be.*
*Author Unknown*

*Dedicated to the Memory of*
*James Allan "Jim" Sanderson*
*and*
*Kevin "Ray" Seely*

## *Leadership is a Reflection of Attitude*

It was difficult to write a humour column when one experiences the loss of friends and local leaders. Forgive me for beginning a humor book with two such sad stories but I wanted to thank these fellows for a lot of laughs and great memories.

We all offer leadership in some way to those around us. Good leaders surround us, but we don't always recognize them as such. We recognize the rich, famous, political, business or self-proclaimed loud leaders but we often overlook the people beside us who provide quiet leadership by example. The people we respect, admire and often look to and who do not demand recognition, so we seldom acknowledge them. The attitude around Grande Prairie's riding community was one of great sadness as they realized the loss of these fine local leaders.

I met **Jim Sanderson**, *(February 14, 1950 to August 12, 2007)* through a local riding club. He warmly welcomed me to the group, and I liked him immediately. Jim, the Vice President of a hospital administration region looked like a biker on the road and the executive leader he was in the boardroom. As the photo shows, he was a mountain of a man, and it took a large man to hold his huge heart. The first time we met, I mentioned how much I liked a patch he was wearing, and the next time we met, he gave me one. On another occasion, I asked where he picked up the vest chains he used, and darned if he didn't come up with a set for me. I know that if we had been granted more time together we would have become great friends, or at least he would have totally outfitted me in riding apparel.

Jim was a successful leader because he knew how to lead by example. He rode cautiously, spoke well of others and had a great sense of humor that set a standard for those who traveled with him. Just knowing him made my life richer.

Jim hit a slippery corner on a ride through the beautiful Canadian Rockies and died from injuries suffered when his bike left the road. My first thought was perhaps it is time to give up riding. If you ride, you will understand why I decided not too after being reminded of the saying, *"A ship is safest in the harbor, but that is not what ships are for."* Jim would have been the first to point that out and encourage us all to enjoy every day we are granted on this earth.

**Kevin "Ray" Seely** died of a tragic motorcycle accident near Lake Louise, Alberta on July 30, 2009.

Born in Grande Prairie on November 15, 1956, Ray spent five years in the Armed Forces where he started his career as a heavy-duty mechanic and leading to the management of a large heavy-duty repair shop. Ray and Shirley settled in Cranbrook, raising their family before moving back to Grande Prairie where Ray discovered his passion for motorcycles. Ray had many friends, some of whom were with him on his final ride.

The riders were behind a pick-up truck when a car crossed the centerline hit the truck and spun into Ray's bike.

When I needed help to install a laminate floor in our Grande Prairie store, a year earlier, Ray offered to help and would not take payment for it. I think of him every time I look at that floor and I will never forget Ray's smile; he was truly a happy and great guy.

*I could not attend Ray's service as I was just released from the hospital suffering from a motorcycle accident.*

# Contents

Introduction . . . . . . . . . . . . . . . . . . . . . . . . . . . . . . . . . . . . . . . xi
1. Deadly Doses . . . . . . . . . . . . . . . . . . . . . . . . . . . . . . . . . . . .1
2. Be Careful What You Ask For . . . . . . . . . . . . . . . . . . . . . . .5
3. Confessions of a Motorcycle Gang . . . . . . . . . . . . . . . . . .11
4. The Bear Facts . . . . . . . . . . . . . . . . . . . . . . . . . . . . . . . . . .15
5. Shiny Things . . . . . . . . . . . . . . . . . . . . . . . . . . . . . . . . . . .17
6. Jesus Saves Souls but... *Loud Pipes Save Lives!* . . . . . . . . .21
7. Jesus to Ride a Suzuki . . . . . . . . . . . . . . . . . . . . . . . . . . . .23
8. The Wave . . . . . . . . . . . . . . . . . . . . . . . . . . . . . . . . . . . . .27
9. Mistress or Motorcycle... You choose. . . . . . . . . . . . . . . .29
10. Alice May be Slack but... *She's Not Easy!* . . . . . . . . . . . . .31
11. Riding the Rockies in April . . . . . . . . . . . . . . . . . . . . . . .33
12. Code of the Road . . . . . . . . . . . . . . . . . . . . . . . . . . . . . . .35
13. Canadian Military Secret Revealed! . . . . . . . . . . . . . . . . .37
14. Spring Run-Off . . . . . . . . . . . . . . . . . . . . . . . . . . . . . . . .39
15. Don't Park –Wright . . . . . . . . . . . . . . . . . . . . . . . . . . . . .41
16. Motivating Teenagers . . . . . . . . . . . . . . . . . . . . . . . . . . . .43
17. Motorcycle Airbags? . . . . . . . . . . . . . . . . . . . . . . . . . . . . .45
18. If You Had to Pick a Bike as a Mate . . . . . . . . . . . . . . . . .47
19. How to Tell a Real Biker . . . . . . . . . . . . . . . . . . . . . . . . . .49
20. *My Obituary* . . . . . . . . . . . . . . . . . . . . . . . . . . . . . . . . . . .51
21. Duke Proctor Dead at 106 . . . . . . . . . . . . . . . . . . . . . . . .53
22. The Back Inversion Machine . . . . . . . . . . . . . . . . . . . . . .55
23. Surprises Kill the Elderly . . . . . . . . . . . . . . . . . . . . . . . . .57

24. Hot Chocolate, Hot Women, Hot Vest . . . . . . . . . . . . . . . . . . .59
25. The Community . . . . . . . . . . . . . . . . . . . . . . . . . . . . . . . . . .61
26. Riding Alone in Cancun . . . . . . . . . . . . . . . . . . . . . . . . . . . .63
27. Riding in the Rain. . . . . . . . . . . . . . . . . . . . . . . . . . . . . . . . .65
28. Protective Wear . . . . . . . . . . . . . . . . . . . . . . . . . . . . . . . . . . .69
29. A Rolling Home Gathers No Moss . . . . . . . . . . . . . . . . . . . .71
30. I'd Rather Be Playing in Traffic! . . . . . . . . . . . . . . . . . . . . . .73
31. e-Bay ... Bidder. . . . . . . . . . . . . . . . . . . . . . . . . . . . . . . . . . .75
32. Jessie James, Outlaws & Bikers . . . . . . . . . . . . . . . . . . . . . . .77
33. Year of the Hog . . . . . . . . . . . . . . . . . . . . . . . . . . . . . . . . . . .79
About the Author . . . . . . . . . . . . . . . . . . . . . . . . . . . . . . . . . . .83
Books by Layton Park . . . . . . . . . . . . . . . . . . . . . . . . . . . . . . . .84

# Introduction

I thought I would start with an apology to anyone who finds some of my stories offensive. I don't set out to insult anyone but sometimes I get in my own way. (No pun intended for my other book, "Get Out Of Your Way.")

Sometimes I say the wrong thing. I don't mean to, I just do.

It's funny how less than five minutes after I join any group the conversation seems to turn to motorcycles. The wife says that I talk about motorcycles too much and that some people may not be interested in them. How sad. We have some evangelizing to do then because everyone should be talking about motorcycles. Even in a book on leadership should have stories relating to motorcycles and thus the title, *"If You Are Going To Lead, Don't Spit."* If you are not a biker just think about it for a while and you will understand the implications. If we understood all the implications in other venues, we would all be better leaders.

The current hot topic, however, seems to be global warming (pun intended). The other day a woman approached me as I was dismounting from my bike and said, "Hello, sonny." This gives you an idea of just how ancient she was. Then turning to my bike, she pointed and said, "It is good to see you riding that. Are you doing it to help defeat global warming?"

"Global warming? Hell, I'm looking forward to the extra riding days global warming will bring us." Apparently, that was not well thought out and was not the right thing to say. It's amazing how fast an old lady can swing a purse.

So is it just me or are we getting a little too politically correct?

I hope you enjoy this book with all its political incorrectness.

Please know that I love to hear from my readers so if you have positive comments enter **"Smart Ass Jack"** in the subject line and send them to me.

Those with critical comments can enter *"Junk"* in the subject line and mail them to any email address as I am working on overcoming one of my weaknesses, trying to please everyone.

May Peter Fonda smile upon you, and may all your rides end shiny side up.

# 1. Deadly Doses

"Unit One, do you see anyone?" A deep voice asked and was answered with a voice that crackled from a two-way radio.

"Nothing here."

I opened my eyes and from my dark room I could see what looked like a black and white monitor in the main room that I was viewing through a small window at the foot of my bed. I tried to move but found I was tied down. I tried to figure out where I was but I had no idea what was happening.

The voice cracked again, "There are headlights at the gate, looks like the sheriff's truck."

"Don't let him come in. We sure don't want him poking around."

"Right," The craggy voice replied.

On the monitor, I could make out a security guard talking to someone in the truck but the voices were low and hard to understand. Then the truck backed up turned and drove away.

"Unit One," the voice crackled.

"Go ahead," the deeper voice responded.

"Seems someone reported a prowler in the neighborhood but I told him no one had crossed our perimeter fence."

"Good, now go find who did cross and make sure they didn't learn anything before you turn them over to the sheriff. We have enough problems with this Canadian here, without someone else getting in our way."

A few minutes after the conversation ended another person came into the main room but like the deep voice, I could not see him. I closed my eyes and listened.

"What is going on?" the newcomer asked.

"The Canadian is still unconscious. We had a break in the perimeter fence but Unit one should have them apprehended soon," Deep Voice said.

"Keep on top of it. We have too much at stake right now and we don't need anyone stumbling into this until we are ready to move."

"Surely we have milked enough money; I think we should get out of here. I am concerned with this new guy here. Some Canadian administrator checking the bills is going to stumble onto something and discover we are not really a hospital and shut down our cash flow."

"Don't worry people die in hospitals every day. I am afraid our new patient will pass away from his injuries soon. We billed almost a quarter million for just his first three days but before they discover the operations were bogus, he will die from the injuries. In any event, this whole operation is going to net us hundreds of millions so we can't get rushed over one lousy foreigner."

I couldn't move I was tied down. I struggled to retain consciousness but drifted off then what seemed like a moment later, there was daylight in my room. I looked around and saw my wife and one of my best friends, Ed. They looked over at me and both smiled as they came to my bedside.

"What the hell is going on?" My voice was weak.

"You were in an accident," Myrna said, "Your bike left the highway and rolled. You broke your neck, your collar bone, your shoulder blade, your arm, all the ribs on your left side and punctured your lung."

"Yes I remember," I tried to move. "Why are my arms tied?"

"The doctors had the nurses tie you because you have been trying to pull your tubes out. Relax, you have been badly injured but you will be okay." She bent over and touched my shoulder.

"Listen," I whispered, "They aren't really doctors. They haven't done anything. I am not injured; I don't feel a thing. This whole set up is a scam."

The wife let out one of her hearty laughs filling the room and spilling out the door. "What are you talking about?" She said.

"Shhh. Look around, for God sake, this is not a hospital. These people are milking insurance companies and the government. They bill for fake operations and treatment and they plan to kill me."

Again she laughed. I was frustrated and lay back for a moment while she walked out the door and began talking to one of the people outside. Then I saw them both look at me and she laughed again. How could she be so foolish not to see it? Now she was telling the very people who were planning to kill me, that I knew their plans. She just speeded them up. I looked over at Ed.

"Ed, come here." I have known Ed for twenty-five years and the fact he'd dropped everything to fly across the country to be with me reminded me just how important our friendship is. He is also very successful and has access to a lot of resources. "Ed, I don't know what is going on but this is not a hospital.

You have to get Myrna out of here she is going to get us all killed. You got to get me out of here and fast." I could feel the panic building.

"Don't worry; I will get on this right away." His voice was reassuring and I calmed as he laid a hand on my shoulder. I knew I could count on him. He called Myrna back to the room then I asked her to leave and go back to the hotel. I said Ed would explain everything. In the meantime, I lay back tied to my bed, completely at the mercy of these people rushing back and forth pretending to be doctors and nurses. I struggled to stay awake but I couldn't and drifted off and somewhere in the darkness; I could hear the sounds of a voice on the radio then nothing.

I awoke again to find Myrna and Ed there.

"What's going on?" I asked, "I thought you were going back to the hotel?"

"That was two days ago." Ed smiled, "You've had another operation but don't worry everything is going to be all right." He looked around as though he was trying not to let anyone else hear then added, "I looked into it myself. This is legitimate."

He didn't get it, I thought. Neither of them realize how big this scam is and what is really going on. Unless... no, Myrna and Ed would never side with these people, it doesn't matter how much money is at stake. They would not give me up for any amount, would they? Then again, a million or two is not much out of an operation that is netting hundreds of millions and for a million dollars who knows what a friend and loved one might do. Am I getting paranoid? Could they be right? Perhaps I misunderstood something. I faded away again.

The next time I woke up, I was in a commercial kitchen. Everyone was sitting around a table when a very large native guy walked in and joined us saying he was the bar manager and his name was Eli. Not only was his size intimidating but also he had two braids that started at the front of his head and ran down each side to the back. Each jet-black braid was woven with a piece of leather and a ribbon of chrome. The conversation turned to the trouble I was having with bowel movements in bed and someone suggested I should get a tube. Trying to be funny, I said I would like chrome ones, like my bike's new pipes.

Eli pointed to some rolls of tubing above the stainless steel counters and I noticed they were a combination of leather and chrome just like his braids. "What about that tubing, it would look good?"

"Yeah," I answered, "But I think there is some health requirements about what gets used."

"It's okay, this tubing is for the bar and the bar falls under the tobacco, liquor and firearms department. They have the same regulations as health care. If it is good enough for the bar, it is good enough for the hospital upstairs."

I was getting nervous but he insisted they could do it in minutes right there on the counter. I finally gave in and the next time I awoke, I had a tube, although I couldn't see what it was made of.

When I tried to discuss it with Ed and the wife, they **both** laughed at me again, apparently not remembering any of it.

I was getting as annoyed as I had been when Myrna refused to call Steven Colbert and Jon Stewart to announce on their shows that I had crashed. A nurse that I had finally began to trust and who was not part of the murder plot came in. I confided in him about my frustration that no one seemed to be taking me seriously.

Very quietly, yet confidently he began to explain how much morphine I was on and its effects. It seems these vivid experiences were simply hallucinations.

In the next moment, I heard the crackly voice from the monitor in the outside room.

"Not that same TV show about the hospital scam? This is the third time it's been on this week," the nurse said and then added, "Will there be anything else?"

"Yes," I answered, "can you get the doctors to change the morphine to a drug that doesn't confuse reality with hallucination?"

☙

**Leaders seldom waste time and energy worrying about fearful or unreal situations created in our mind.**
**Remember FEAR is False Events Appearing Real.**

# 2. Be Careful What You Ask For

Have you ever woke up to a milestone birthday and wondered what you had accomplished? Are you on the right path? Are you making a difference? When I turned 60, I asked myself those questions and it was then that I decided to take a ride around America, alone and contemplate the answer. I traded in my two older motorcycles for a new one and set out.

Day three started out with a light rain, towards noon the sky cleared as the miles rolled by, the Nevada desert becoming more desolate and barren. The air stirred a little, but the breeze felt more like a blast of hot air from a furnace than relief. There was little traffic on the road explaining why it is called "the loneliest highway in the world."

One moment I was enjoying the ride through this desert then suddenly there was nothingness. I could not feel the hot sand that covered my face. Nor could I feel my broken neck, smashed shoulder blade, crushed collarbone, the broken ball and socket in the shoulder joint, my punctured lung or all my crushed ribs. I experienced no feelings, saw no white light, no tunnel nor did I hear a single angel sing. I just lay there; face down not breathing, immersed in a vast black emptiness.

Calvin Nelson, a biker from Pasco, Washington, was following me on his motorcycle when he saw me leave the road in a cloud of dust. He quickly stopped and parked his bike on the side of the highway and ran down into the ditch to the crash site. He carefully rolled me over and quickly undid the top buttons on of my jacket and shirt. Somewhere inside the pile of cells that connect together making up my physical body, a light flickered and the spirit that resides inside, giving us all the magic of life, caused me to take a breath. The light of life flickered again, and I took another breath and it was then that Spirit within me decided, this would not be my last day.

As Calvin worked on me, he heard the rare sound of a car, and ran back up the sandy slope. He stood right in the middle of the road waving so the car had to stop. He asked the woman, a nurse as it turned out, to call 911 then he ran back quickly followed by the nurse carrying a pillow and blanket. They were both surprised to see me on my knees trying to stand and gently, but firmly, talked me into lying back down to wait for an ambulance.

I don't remember much of what followed until I woke up four days and three operations later in the trauma unit of Renown Medical Center, in Reno, somehow knowing that this rider's life was forever changed.

As I tried to assess where I was I realized my wife was holding my hand. She said, "You have been in a terrible accident but you don't have brain or spinal cord injuries. We can deal with everything else, so just relax and let the doctors take care of you."

I could hear a patient screaming in a nearby room and the health care provider shouted back telling him to hold still. It seemed that no matter how loud the caregiver yelled, *"relax",* it didn't work.

Then a doctor walked into my room with a tube saying he had to put it up my nose in order to drain my lung. I felt my wife squeeze my hand and recoil at the mention of it.

The last dozen years I have been using hypnosis to help people control their minds and I wrote the book, *Get Out of Your Way,* summarizing how to remove our limiting fears and beliefs in order to overcome the emotions that hold us back. I teach the power of focus and mental strength to overcome pain, sickness, fear and addictions.

I had worked with hundreds of clients and most told me my services helped them achieve their goals. Instead of being grateful for being able to help so many clients, I had recently begun to ask the questions, "Are I making a difference?" As I focused on these doubts, I began to get in my own way and questioning my effectiveness.

Like many of us, I began to take responsibly for things I could not control. I began to question the value of my services, thinking all I really did was talk to the clients. It's not like I had a tangible tool, a magic wand or could produced visual change.

The doctors who performed surgery on me left me fingerprints of their work on the outside and inside of my body. There are scars from the incisions across my neck, back and shoulder and on the inside there is plating on my ribs that show up in x-rays. The work I do with my clients leaves no visible marks.

My inner voice kept asking, "How can you be sure your work is really helping? How would I know if I was really making a difference?" I began asking for a sign that it did indeed make a difference.

One-theory states if you ask, an answer will be provided, but I wasn't prepared for the loud response I was now receiving.

It was as though this motorcycle accident was to provide me an opportunity to use my mind and face my own fears. My fears included pain, needles and tubes going in or out of my body. Would I be able to take my own advice? Could I get out of my way?

Before my accident I had just completed the first draught of my book "Spirit Doctor" the hypnotic healings of Quimby [Phineas Parkhurst Quimby- Father of New Thought] and many of Phineas's words came back to me during my stay in the Renown Medical Center, with much more significance and substance.

As the doctor continued to prepare his hose, it occurred to me that the medical staff was going to do whatever they felt necessary in order to save and repair me and my protesting or screaming, like the man next door, would not change that.

I knew they might plug off my airways or make me uncomfortable for a short period of time but curing me did not include suffocating me, so whatever they did, it would not be for long. I looked at my wife again and knew even in my drug-induced state, that she would never allow them to do anything that was going to hurt me in the long term. I also knew the more relaxed all my muscles were, the easier the procedures would be.

It was at that moment I made the conscious decision to relax and use self-hypnosis. I closed my eyes and imagined that I could see the profile of my good friend Dr. Kenn Gordon, director of our spiritual center and president of the International Centers for Spiritual Living. I remembered conversations we had on this very subject. It was as though the sun was shinning on the profile of his face and his smile gave me peace.

In that moment, I knew that Dr. Kenn my trusted spiritual director would be asking hundreds of people to pray to Spirit, God, Universal Intelligence or whatever each person calls their creator to help and take care of me through this challenging time.

In the next breath I relaxed and slipped into a deep hypnotic state. I focused on a promising future and surrendered to the medical staff, allowing them to do whatever they wanted, knowing I would come out the other side feeling better than ever. I also promised myself that when they were finished, I would thank them and tell them how much I appreciated everything they were doing no matter how uncomfortable it was for me.

Later Myrna and some of the staff said they could not believe how brave I was as I just laid there and let them stick hoses in me time after time to suck fluids from my lungs. The truth is, I was not brave at all but selfish. I knew the easier I was to deal with and the more grateful I was towards the medical team, the more they would want to work with me and the gentler they would treat me. I knew if I focused, I could handle anything.

Thinking about this I decided my job was to be the team leader, and as such, I was to provide encouragement and the best working environment I could for these tireless professionals. I relaxed, focused and thanks to self-hypnosis, (and some of the drugs I am sure) I never really felt pain.

At 6'3" and 280 lbs, I would be best described as the biggest crybaby when it comes to hospitals, so if I can focus my mind to overcome pain and fear, then anyone can. With practice you can change anything you desire.

At one point near the end of my stay, a nurse came in to take blood samples saying, "This will only sting for a moment."

"Sting?" I said looking at her, "I didn't come here to be stung, to be hurt or feel pain. You should tell me, "This may be a little uncomfortable for a moment but that is all."

She looked at me like I was crazy or out of my mind with the drugs. She poked the needle in three times without being able to find a vein or get a single drop of blood. I told her not to worry as this often happens to which she responded, "Why didn't you tell me so I could be prepared?"

"Prepared for what? To fail?" I said, "Had I told you this was often a problem you would expect it to be a problem and I wanted you to expect it would work the first time." She stared at me, obviously not understanding my response or the Law of Expectation. As she continued to look at me with a jaundiced eye, she called for another nurse. When the new nurse entered, I said, "I heard you are the best at getting blood,"

She smiled and said, "I don't know if I am the best, but I am pretty darn good." Smiling, she pushed the needle in and hit a producer on the first hole.

I teach the mental laws and how they work so why had I been surprised when they worked for me?

During my stay in ICU, I experienced no real pain, very little discomfort and soon I had the staff kibitzing and laughing with me. Often because I had too many tubes in my throat to talk and they couldn't read the notes on my trusty clip board or understand my Canadian slang.

Late Saturday night just after the third operation my heart began to race. The doctors called Myrna to come in early Sunday morning and told her to prepare herself to lose me because in addition to all my broken bones and punctured lung, I now had pneumonia.

Myrna is the most positive person I have ever met. Through her professional speaking she had met the Spiritual Directors of the Centres for Spiritual Living in Tucson, Phoenix, and Reno, and that morning she emailed them, our own Centre, and all the bikers who had been sending us messages of encouragement. She asked for prayer and healing treatments and that Sunday morning, numerous people around the US and Canada, said morning prayers asking for my health to be returned.

Myrna and I are not religious people, but we believe in one universal mind and the power of spirit, so when the new "pneumonia" test results came back that afternoon she was not surprised they were negative. Given my symptoms and condition, there was no logical explanation for it, unless of course, the Law of Mind was at work!

When Myrna and I left the Reno trauma unit nineteen days later, over thirty staff lined up to wish us well and watch the paramedics wheel me out to the one hundred and thirty thousand dollar Lear Jet the insurance company paid for, complete with an ER doctor, a trauma nurse and a respiratory therapist to accompanied us home. It seems the medical insurance company, was even more anxious than I was to get me back to Canada and free health care.

I did nothing heroic or special, I just decided that I would not experience pain and instead I would focus on and enjoy being alive and I did. Not only did the Reno experience begin the healing of my body, it began the healing of my mental doubt.

I did not give in to the hot sands. I did not die and return, I was reawakened to the magnificence of the universal mind and my mental connection to it. My experience gave me confidence in my work and the words of Phineas Parkhurst Quimby. (See my book Spirit Doctor the hypnotic healings of Quimby)

*"There is nothing animate in the body, so when the body is injured by what we call disease, it is by an error of the mind, the body being subject to the mind, so when the mind is corrected of its error, the truth is established which is its health."*
P. H. **Quimby** *1802-1866*

༄

***So be careful what you ask for...***
***Your mind will take you seriously!***

*Col. Layton Park*

*"As you can see, Layton's motorcycle accident left him with all the bones on the left side of his body crushed...
I guess you could say he is all right now!"*

Who would have known that Myrna could write such a beautiful and funny account of my hospital adventure? She had over 17,000 hits on the blog, BackRoadScholar .com and along with all the responses from readers; it has become a large book in itself.

We will have these articles put into an e-book soon but unfortunately will have to edit out a number of the responses to shorten it. If you would like a copy just email *laytonpark@shaw.ca* and put the Reno adventure in the subject line. Thanks all for the support.

*Everyone crashes. Some get back on. Some don't. Some can't.*
*- Author Unknown*

# 3. Confessions of a Motorcycle Gang

Highway 40 winds through the foothills of the Canadian Rockies as though the engineers designed it specifically for motorcycles. It could not have had more corners if the plans had been drawn using 'Etch-a-sketch. My bike loved the hills and easily hugged the road as I followed an old friend and his buddy.

My friend, who I will call Chuck for the purposes of this story, makes a great biker, as he comes from an intimidating profession that strikes fear in the hearts of many. He is a car salesman. However, a local bylaw prohibiting the wearing of colours prevents him from wearing a plaid suit when we ride.

His buddy, also on the north side of 50, is not a hard-core biker either but has watched *Easy Rider* a dozen times. This guy chose a bike based on the most horsepower he could buy. He scorned the thought of driving a comfortable, big, laid-back cruiser. You could hardly see the small crotch-rocket underneath him, which he rides in the customary facedown, fetal position.

The nine-thousand horsepower it produces at a million RPM means he can go from 0 to 150 kilometers an hour in first gear in three seconds, a feature he does not exercise to its fullest, as he does not have enough underwear. However, it was still enough to earn him the nickname "Speed."

As well as owning a car dealership, my friend, Chuck, also owns a motorcycle shop, so when it came to accessories, he had at least one of everything. He was proud of the immaculate older touring bike the shop had rebuilt to showroom condition for almost as little as the cost of a new home. His only complaint was a very small pinhole in the paint, which he had to point out in order for it to be seen.

"Can you believe that?" He said in disgust. "My own body shop, and now I have to have them repaint the back fender."

For this ride, he wore new leathers and a pair of new riding boots, which he kept staring at and saying we should all buy a pair. One of the problems with wearing protective leather, especially chaps or pants, is once they're zipped it's impossible to bend any joints. My friend suggested the problem is compounded by wearing jeans, most of which are built like a cheap hotel. His dealership, on the other hand, sold only first-class stretchy jeans.

*Col. Layton Park*

He said the stretchy jeans with spandex in the crotch and knees, help his joints move easier, although his sons did not want to be seen in public with him when he was wearing them. Now all dressed up and on the road, we looked more like the three caballeros than real bikers, and I say that meaning no disrespect to our Mexicans readers.

These readers will know that the one thing all cheap hotels have in common is no ballroom, but I digress.

Following my friend on the road, I leaned into one turn after another, then noticed the highway engineer had built one more corner than my friend was prepared to negotiate… or perhaps he was still admiring his boots. Either-way, at that moment he was about to earn the nickname "Ditch."

Ditch's motorcycle left the road in style, launching off the high side of the curve. Like a bull rider, he managed to ride it all the way to the bottom, displaying the demeanor of a rag doll. The front wheel stopped abruptly when it dropped into a deep drainage cut. Ditch did not.

Thankfully, the area was a combination of marsh and moss, making his landing spectacular, yet soft. The news flashed through the wildlife population. Now whenever you come upon a deer in the area, it freezes, as thought caught in the proverbial headlights, not sure whether to risk staying in the middle of the road or to run for the weeds where Ditch might hit it.

We dug the bike out of the mud and pulled the tall grass and weeds off it. The bike had escaped miraculously with only a couple of scrapes, a broken cowling and mirror. As Ditch tried to clean the bike off, I tried to offer encouragement by suggesting that the pinhole wasn't as noticeable now.

After pushing the bike back up the hill and onto the road, we needed a break. That is when we decided to charter our own motorcycle gang, but could not agree on a name. Ditch thought we should name it to honor our drug of choice, which he freely dispensed to us at every stop, but we felt it too hard to say Ibuprofen.

The Motrin Cycles was determined to be too commercial, and we felt no one would respect the name Anacin or Aspirin Angels.

We headed out again, and it began to rain, each of us toughing it out alike the rugged bikers we are. Ditch and Speed pulled on their full-face helmets and reduced the speed on their cruise controls. Speed turned on his heated seat and handle grips to keep warm. Ditch sat back on his two-wheel couch and mumbled something about forgetting his battery-operated socks and shorts as he plugged in his heated vest. I continued shivering on my twenty-five-year-old ride, my face hidden behind a three-dollar bandana to minimize the sting of the rain.

The trip continued through the spectacular Banff-Jasper Parkway, then along the Trans-Canada to the Okanagan. The rest of the trip through the Rockies was magnificent, wet and uneventful.

Sometimes at night, just as I am about to fall asleep, I can hear highway 40 calling me north. I can imagine cruising the curves again with Ditch and Speed, which relaxes me and makes it easy to fall asleep.

If you have never ridden through the Canadian Rockies or with Ditch and Speed, I urge you to do so, as either event is a great adventure.

*A lack of focus will cause problems anywhere...
not just while riding your motorcycle.
Spend as much time in the now as possible.
Had I learned this lesson from Ditch...
I may have avoided my own ditch encounter.*

Col. Layton Park

## Thought from the Ditch

*That's all the motorcycle is, a system of concepts worked out in steel.*
*Robert M. Pirsig, Zen and the Art of Motorcycle Maintenance*

*Most motorcycle problems are caused by the nut that connects the handlebars to the saddle.*
*~Author Unknown*

*It takes more love to share the saddle than it does to share the bed.*
*~Author Unknown*

*Bikes don't leak oil, they mark their territory.*
*~Author Unknown*

*Keep your bike in good repair: motorcycle boots are not comfortable for walking.*
*~Author Unknown*

*The best alarm clock is sunshine on chrome.*
*~Author Unknown*

Ditch

# 4. The Bear Facts

To ninety-nine percent of the world, traveling though the Canadian Rockies is considered the exotic dream of a lifetime, and the few who do it on a bike experience the ultimate ride.

The one percent of us who do it on a regular basis not only fail to enjoy it, we are often in too big a hurry to notice the beauty. It's not that we don't want to look, it's just that the hills and corners require concentration when you're traveling at a buck sixty. The big danger of traveling at that speed is you also have to keep glancing in the mirror to make sure a sports bike doesn't run into you from behind. It's not that the sixteen-year-old riders are not good riders; it's just that they can't always maneuver around you when the front wheel is six feet off the ground. Besides, it's hard for them to brake quickly without losing their flip-flops.

On one of my regular trips, I decided to take an extra day, slow down and enjoy the experience. I headed north from Kamloops on the Yellowhead Highway, stopping at antique stores in Barrier and Old Fort with a stop at the UFO ice cream store before pressing on.

Blue River is not the end of the world, but you can see it from there. I was riding alone on a quiet stretch of highway when I noticed ahead a large brown bear, standing on the white line looking straight at me. I geared down and began slowing, waiting for the bear to head for the trees as they usually do, but this bear stood his ground. I thought perhaps I could get onto the shoulder of the road and gun by him, but he would be close, and if he bolted for the wrong ditch, a collision with a bear would not be a good thing.

I geared down again and wished I had louder pipes as my stock mufflers barked slightly but not enough to move the bear. I thought of the pepper spray I had backed in my tee-bag. A lot of good it is doing there, I thought. As I continued to watch him, our eyes locked, and I rolled to a stop about sixty feet away. I was sure I could spin the bike and accelerate before he reached me, but I still felt a little naked, standing and staring at that creature. After what seemed like an eternity, he moved to the opposite shoulder, still maintaining eye contact.

I released the clutch and began slowly rolling up the shoulder. The bear didn't move until I was opposite him. Then he broke eye contact and lumbered into the trees. I breathed easier and rumbled down the road.

The experience made me question the value of bear bells and it reminded me that the way they tell the difference between black bear and grizzly bear droppings is that grizzly droppings smell like pepper and have bells in it.

On a previous sunny, warm, spring morning, I had encountered a pair of grizzlies on the highway just south of Jasper. I rounded the corner and rolled to a stop a hundred feet short of the two huge creatures. The silver one slowly looked up as he lay on the warm pavement. I thought I detected the kind of a smile that might come after an encounter during mating season.

The big dark female eased herself into a standing position and glanced at me, the newcomer, then grunted at her mate. I thought I understood her to say, "Did you order meals on wheels?"

He continued to lay there too tired to move, studying my leathers and helmet. He returned the grunt as if to say, "No, I find fast food to tough for me."

"They really aren't bad once you strip away the tough outer hide and crack open the top shell," was her reply.

He considered it, but neither seemed to have enough energy to bother with me. Finally, she decided to go down to the stream to enjoy a cold bath. He watched her for a moment, and then swaggered after her.

Only on a motorcycle can you really enjoy this type of experience, and believe it or not, these sightings are not unique. I seldom make this run without seeing a bear, and I always see deer, moose, elk, coyotes and the occasional wolf.

When I arrive in Jasper, I always relax at Crystal's Cozy Accommodation, a very comfortable bed and breakfast, before pushing on, feeling sorry for the ninety-nine percent that can only dream of such a trip.

*❧*

**Give your mind the rest it deserves as often as possible by finding some way to spend time enjoying nature.**

# 5. Shiny Things

When I bought a new motorcycle, I looked at every make and model, studied the specifications, and checked out the reliability, the prices and how well they held their resale value. Then armed with all this information, I bought the one with the most chrome although I didn't know why; I did it at the time. After all, I now have to spend as much time shining it as I do riding it but for some reason I'm attracted to it.

Choices in motorcycles have come along way from having the choice between buying a black bike, completely covered in shiny new grease and oil, or an older black bike covered with a layer of dull dust stuck to duller grease and oil. It was as though something in my genes forced me to choose the shiny one, even if it might not remain that way.

Finally, my fourteen-year-old philosopher son, Liam, cleared the mystery for me. A young teenage lady invited him to a birthday party, and he asked if I would drive him down to the mall to buy her a present. I asked what he was going to buy her, and he said, "I don't know, I'll just find something shiny, because girls are like birds. They like shiny things."

So there it is. I am genetically attracted to shiny things, not because I like them but because I am programmed to do so in order to perpetuate the species. Thanks, son! Isn't it scary that he discovered that at such a young age and had to explain it to his father? I guess that explains why he is kid number five. Good thing for him I didn't discover the secret for myself fifteen-years ago and quit giving his mother shiny things. It may also explain where all the spare change from the dresser goes and why even though my head is beginning to get shinier, she still likes me. But as my old English teacher would say, again I digress.

If I may wander for a moment longer, it pleases me to think how it would freak the old teach out if she actually knew I was now writing as a career. Best of all, I do it breaking all the old rules she taught me and some folks still read it. Maybe I should start an outlaw writing gang. It just goes to show you that you should never let someone else's option affect your plans to pursue your dreams.

So, what else have we learned today? We now know that once again it is women's fault that we have to spend so much money buying chrome things for our bikes. We men pretend we are doing it for ourselves. The truth is, if a couple of good-looking women showed up at the local coffee shop then walked past all the shiny hardware and asked some goofus on a dull green, oil-leaking, World War II Russian army surplus bike if they could have a ride. All the other men would immediately be at the war surplus store trading in their bikes for the same kind.

But never fear – that won't happen, because women know the power of shiny and that men can be tricked. They understand how the shiny theory works. They let us have the shiny bikes as tokens of their appreciation, since they know they can get better shiny things just by winking. They want shiny in the range of diamond rings and necklaces. Men don't completely grasp the theory, which is why so many of us buy them new shiny stainless steel appliances instead then wonder why we have to spend the night on the not-so-shiny couch.

This is an important lesson, men. Trust me. I know this, not because I am a sage but because I have bought a lot of shiny things for my wife. They were good things, too, like the used ski-doo I bought her for Christmas, the thirty-year-old Yamaha motorcycle I gave to her for Mother's Day, the new boat motor for Valentine's Day, and the tent trailer for her birthday. I still don't understand why she turned her nose up at that last one. I'm sure she could have repaired the canvas if she had really tried. Anyway, these gifts generated alone nights on the couch, during which time I contemplated the theory.

Shiny things are good, so buy all the chrome you want, but don't buy shiny things as a gift for the wife unless she can wear it. This point really hit home with me last Fathers Day when the wife gave me a shiny new present. If any of you boys want to see a German-made stainless steel washing machine drop by the house this weekend, where I will be polishing it before I wax my ride.

☙

*If You Are Going to Lead... Don't Spit!*

*Liam Park and Boulevard 90 Motorcycle*

**Never underestimate the wisdom of young and inexperienced minds, as they too seem to have the ability to tap into universal truths.**

*If a warped mind such as mine, can read into or interpret this from the Good Book, then perhaps we should question every event or statement we hear or read. Always research, evaluate and think, then draw your own conclusions.*

# 6. Jesus Saves Souls but…
## *Loud Pipes Save Lives!*

The Good Book say's, "David's Triumph could be heard throughout the land." That would only be possible if David's Triumph motorcycle had loud pipes and if it was good enough for David, need I say more? I will prove in this article that he had loud pipes not because of the slogan "loud pipes save lives" but because he could pick up more women.

I do have a word or two to say on the subject of loud pipes and like everyone else that comments on the subject, I will not let the lack of facts stand in the way of my opinion.

*"I geared down and began slowing waiting for the bear to head for the trees as they usually do, but he stood his ground. I thought perhaps I could get onto the shoulder and gun by him, but he would be close, and if he bolted for the wrong ditch, a collision with a bear would not be a good thing. I geared down again and* **wished I had louder pipes** *as my stock mufflers barked slightly but not enough to move the bear."*

If you read the chapter "Bear Facts," you will know that I survived that experience, as though the writing of this book wasn't clue enough for you. There are other examples of how loud pipes can save lives, and not just lives of humans but the bears, deer and other wildlife we come upon while riding in the Great White North.

For some time I've been testing the theory (by keeping my stock pipes) that loud pipes save lives by letting drivers know when a biker is nearby. I have discovered, though, that when I drive in the city, automobile drivers (unlike bears) seldom make eye contact. Most are so immersed in their own thoughts or reading their text messages that they don't notice bikers, so perhaps it is time to really examine this question.

I know there have been no studies or evidence that loud pipes do save lives, but I have often seen people in the right lane begin making a lane change without noticing I'm riding beside them. I'm sure if my bike had a deep, low rumble, the drivers who use the brail keys at the drive-through ATMs might at least hear me.

The problem, as I see it, is the distinction between a bike that rumbles nice and deep near the legal 91-decibel level, and the obnoxious straight pipes that belt out an ear-splitting bark in excess of a hundred decibels. The louder bikes may let more people know we are in the same city, but half the drivers react by wanting to run all bikers down rather than avoid us.

This conclusion is based on a study I conducted in which I asked two other people for their opinion of loud vehicles. This included a homeboy with a five-hundred-dollar car powered by the vibrations of his ten-thousand-dollar stereo. A stereo that constantly belts out what sounds like the same song which sounds similar to an angry tribe drumming as they prepare to attack at first light. Yet he doesn't like the loud sounds of a motorcycle. Of course, like all polls, this study is accurate within a range of five percent, nineteen times out of twenty, based solely on my opinion.

The real reason men prefer loud vehicles has little to do with safety and, like shiny things, is purely the fault of women. Men have only one motivation, and that is to discover the best way to impress women. We have been doing it since the start of time, and loud pipes are just another way of beating our chest and grunting loudly. Women notice loud vehicles. Have you ever heard a woman tell another, "I really dig the guy on the moped? He is so quiet you can barely hear him. That is so cool." No, they hang out with the loud guys.

If women got excited and started dating men driving quiet four-cylinder KIAs, not only would the world be a quieter place, but there would be no energy crisis. If you want a world full of quieter vehicles, then women, it is up to you: run out and hit on the next guy you see driving a hybrid. When that starts happening, it won't take long before all men will be driving one.

I can prove this because the bible also states that, "the Apostles were all in one Accord." We all know that Hondas are quiet, and we know the apostles didn't have any women. The Good Book also says, "Jehovah drove Adam and Eve out of the Garden in a Fury." Ford brags that the Fury is as quiet as a Mercedes, but despite this big endorsement, you don't hear women being impressed by men who cruise around in them.

Not only did David have the only loud bike in the Bible, he also had over 400 wives and concubines. So there you have it: the Good Book clearly makes the connection between loud pipes and lots of women. No wonder guys want their rides loud.

# 7. Jesus to Ride a Suzuki

The question that seems to come up a lot is, "If Jesus returned to earth today, what bike would he ride?" If that question isn't coming up in your circle, your friends are not contemplating the important things in life.

I know this question hits a nerve with the Christian bikers as I can hear you yelling from here, that the query is blasphemous. I'm sure you feel I will be struck down by lighting, and I don't mean a BSA Lighting 650.

To even suggest Jesus would ride anything but a Harley is blasphemy to many of you, even though angels from the dark side prefer that bike as well. A Harley is somehow considered holy by both sides and to suggest Jesus ride anything less in many a mind is unthinkable. Some may feel he could come back on *"Harley the Lesser,"* a Buell, because it's today's mule.

There is little doubt John the Baptist would be a hard-core Harley rider, and probably Peter as well, but I think John and James would choose duel sport bikes, as they were both fishermen. Paul, on the other hand, was blinded on the road to Damascus, indicating he was probably riding something with a lot of chrome bling, which, of course, had to be a cruiser. Before you write to tell me that Paul was never apart of the original gang my editor already pointed that out, I am just saying what I think his choice of ride would be.

But why would Jesus choose a Suzuki? Isn't it obvious? He would want to have a bike that had the creative style of America yet the fine workmanship of the rising sun, thereby bringing together the best of East and West.

I don't expect you to just take my word for it. Why not attend church this weekend, and when you shake hands with the preacher, ask him "What bike do you think Christ would ride if he returned to earth today?" I'm sure that will open up a very lively conversation.

> *This proves that there is no point or sense to all articles*
> *Have you read things that made no sense, but some how*
> *Every one is encouraged to suspend his or her belief*
> *and be influenced by them?*
> *Leaders question everything.*

Col. Layton Park

*Nevada Hotel in the rain the morning of the crash*

*If you don't ride in the rain, you don't ride. ~ Anonymous*

*If You Are Going to Lead... Don't Spit!*

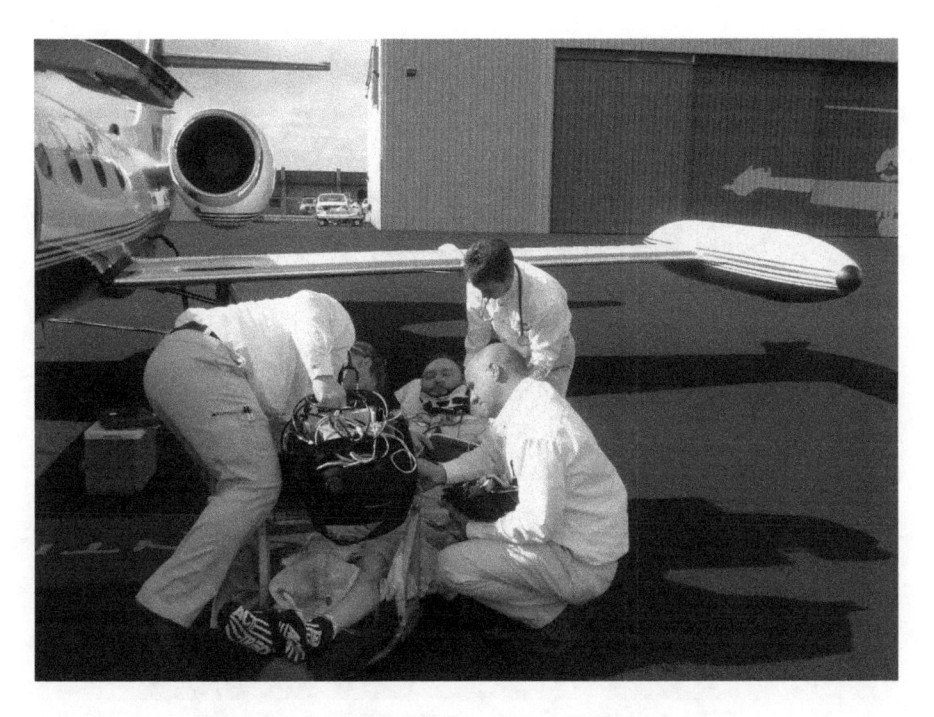

*Leaving on a jet plane... than god for insurance!*

*Never ride faster than your guardian angel can fly.*
*-Author Unknown*

*Col. Layton Park*

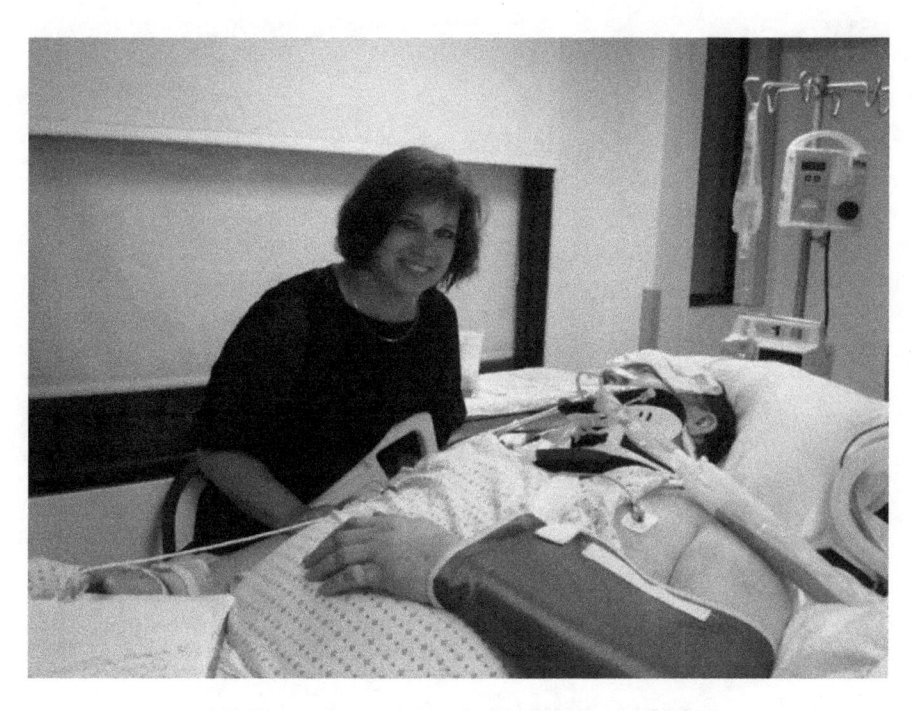

*Myrna and Layton in the Reno Trauma Unit*

*Never argue with the Ditch. ~ C. Longmate*

# 8. The Wave

I started riding a bike in 1964 but after being away for a few years found a lot of new bikes, bikers and habits had developed.

One of the most important is the wave. I was excited to see so many more bikes on the road that I began waving to everyone, but not everyone waved back. Then I discovered there is a protocol to waving, and not everyone is aware of it, so I thought I'd pass along what I have learned.

First of all, new bikers and old fools, all wave like the queen. You know, open upright hand swaying back and forth like it is sitting on top of a spring. Some modify the wave by cupping the hand and giving it a slight figure eight. If you do not mind looking like a queen, fill your boots, but be warned you are only one step away from riding sidesaddle.

I found that dirt bike riders don't wave at all. The only time I see them is when they are leaping from ditch to ditch across the road and the only things attached to the bike is their hands. I can't say I blame them. Besides, with all the mud on the goggles, they probably can't see you anyway.

Older riders tend to avert their eyes from the crotch rockets, unless they are having a deep mid-life crisis, have ignored their back specialist, and are riding one as well. Of course, crotch rockets don't wave either, because each bike comes with a young lady wearing a thong, hanging on for dear life, penetrating her fingers so far into the rib cage that the driver can't let go of his handle bars.

A word of caution: if you do buy a sports bike, be kind to your female friends, and don't offer them a ride unless they're anorexic. These bikes are not flattering, and even the thinnest woman will look wider than a hay wagon from the rear. The full view of the thong really doesn't help either.

Some feel these riders are both too young and too cool to wave, but they really are just holding on so tight they can't let go. Besides, they're in a hurry and hell-bent for the crash site. Moreover, most of them are folded over the tank, trying to reach the bars, unable to bend their head up far enough to even see you wave at them.

If you ride one of these bikes, please don't write in to complain about these comments, as I'm just passing along what I have learned. I have nothing against low bars. In fact, I frequent them on occasion. Since I am a pilot as well as a rider, I really do understand the reluctance to wave. Any change in the aerodynamics of a machine traveling near the speed of sound can have devastating effects, more serious than just blowing your tank-top and sandals off. At least most of these riders wear the best in helmets and full-face protection, so after the accident their service can have an open casket from the shoulders up.

The old boys with the attitude "Hey, look at my new cruiser" are always generous with their waves and come in two categories. The first is the I-will-just-raise-my-wrist-from-the-bars-and-flash-a-couple-of–fingers-to-show-I'm-a-cool-biker-now-but-not-so-obvious-I'll-feel-foolish-if-I-don't-get-a-wave-back.

The second is the straight-arm-to-five-o'clock. Here the index finger can be used alone, or better yet the thumb and two forefingers. These are real bikers… you can tell by the freshly ironed dew rag, new shiny leathers, and a pin they picked up at Sturgis right after they unloaded their bike and parked the trailer. The accessories help disguise the fact these mean biker dudes are often chartered accountants, lawyers, stock brokers or nurses from the local old-age home. All the same, they are all enjoying the pleasures of the open road and welcome anyone to join them, so wave back. It is one of the few times you can actually afford to communicate with these guys.

Finally, there is the "I am a real – and I mean **real** – mean outlaw biker dude." These are only found on Harleys or stolen bikes. They only wave at other Harleys, which is getting more difficult because it is hard to identify the make of any cruiser style approaching with a passing speed of 200 kilometers per hour. Even parked, it has become almost impossible to tell the different cruisers apart, as the Japanese now build bikes that look more like Harleys, and Harley now builds bikes that no longer leave the old telltale signature on the pavement. There has never been a better time to be bikers, as all the manufacturers now build good-looking, good-sounding and reliable machines. But again, I digress.

The outlaws prefer to use the low straight-arm technique or the one finger salute. While the queen wears a forced smile in waving, these bikers wear a forced scowl. On the road, they are part of the two-wheel fraternity, and parking your bike next to theirs usually, guarantees that you can leave your helmet unlocked on the bike, as passer-byers will not dare mess with it and the outlaws have no use for one.

In the next chapter, we will discuss how to gracefully ask for help after you fail to extend your kickstand all the way and the bike falls over trapping you underneath as you get off. In the meantime, keep the shiny side up.

# 9. Mistress or Motorcycle… You choose.

One Saturday morning in March, I rolled over and explained to my wife that the mid-fifties itch was bothering me and would it be okay if I got a mistress.

"I don't think so!" was her short reply, so I countered with, "Well how do you feel about a new motorcycle then?"

I'd like to think it was my savvy negotiating skills that allowed me to close that deal and get a new bike. The truth is she was already ahead of me. She knew I could probably still handle a motorcycle. She suggested I look into buying Ditch's demo, which I had spoken of fondly. The wife has always encouraged me to do things I enjoy, and she knew I would really enjoy the 2,200 kilometers I put on every month going from Kelowna to Grande Prairie, if I had a good ride.

The old Yamaha never let me down, but given the miles of nothing but remote bush, the thought sometimes bothered me that I could get stranded out there. Then one day I came upon a Harley rider that was broken down by the side of the road. I stopped and said, "You need any help?"

"Yeah, do you have a wrench?" he answered. "Sure," I said, opening my saddlebag. "What size do you need?"

"A big one," he replied. "I want to use it as a hammer to beat this piece of…"

I then could picture myself stuck in the same predicament, with my only mechanical skill the ability to beat the living crap out of the bike if it should fail. This incident was my wake-up call.

I liked the thought of having a reliable bike, and soon I was on the new Boulevard. The wife even began riding with me, and we enjoyed a number of good rides together.

On one occasion, an infected tooth forced us to interrupt a trip. My wife walked into the dentist's office in the small town we passed through, and the dentist walked up to the front counter. "I want a tooth pulled, and I don't want to waste any time with pain killers because we're in a big hurry," said the wife.

The dentist started to say something, but she cut him off, saying, "Look, just pull the tooth as quick as possible and we'll be on our way."

The dentist stared at her with his mouth half open for a moment, then said, "Wow. You are one tough woman. Which tooth is it?"

The wife turned to me and said, "Show him your tooth, dear."

Eventually we were ready to see how the wife would handle a longer ride, so we set out for Calgary. After the 700-kilometer trip, she said she might feel more comfortable on her own bike, and so the shopping began. Although she had a dirt bike twenty years ago, she let her license lapse. She felt she should start out with something small, get her new license and then see how she feels in traffic. Within days, she was easily riding an older Honda 250 Elite scooter.

I am feeling so lucky to have a new bike, a new biking partner, as well as a great wife (not necessarily in that order... the wife should be ahead of the biking partner). I thought I should share my secret techniques on how to negotiate a new bike so perhaps you can use them.

By using the Layton Mistress-or-Motorcycle Negotiating System, you, too, will soon find yourself on a new bike. If you already have a bike, then using my method of taking her on an eight-hour trip will result in her falling in love with biking and wanting a bike of her own.

Warning: results may vary from wife to wife, and I cannot accept liability if neither technique works for you. Occasionally you may risk side effects, such as finding extra riding time following the divorce. You may no longer have enough money to buy gas for the bike, but that's okay because she will own it anyway.

Other side effects may include prolonged periods of silence or shivering cold and alone on the couch all night or feeling subjected to intense conversations in which you do not get a chance to speak.

These risks are worth experiencing the sheer joy of riding in the wind with the best-possible riding partner, your wife.

***

*You should have gotten the point of this article without my pointing out the following:*
1. *All negotiations should begin with an outrageous opening gambit.*
2. *A bike is cheaper to acquire than a mistress, it is less expensive to maintain and it is less of a problem when you drop it.*

# 10. Alice May be Slack but…
## *She's Not Easy!*

I decided to take my new ride from Grande Prairie, Alberta to Penticton, B.C. for the Slack Alice Show and Shine in early April. As if on queue, it began raining as I pulled away from the city. I decided there was no need to put on the rain suit as the weather channel said the route was to be sunny, some clouds and a chance of light showers. I should have remembered that weathermen and economists are interchangeable as neither is based in reality. After two hours of very wet sunshine followed by low sleet-laden clouds interrupted by blowing snow, I changed my mind and finished dressing.

The new Boulevard performed great with the exception of the range. My dealer (the guy known as Ditch, who not only sold me the bike but provides all the ibuprofen I need for free) said it should reach Grande Cache (the only sign of civilization on this remote road through the Canadian North) with no problem. Of course, now he claims he meant if I drove it less than a buck twenty. Big bike, big highway, big boy – why would I not use big speed? The closer I got, the faster I rode, thinking I could get there before it ran out of gas… Big mistake.

Ten kilometers out of Grande Cache, I was watching the empty light flash when the deafening sound of silence hit me. There was a small field to the left, and well below the highway and I could see a couple of trailers camped with quads on the back of their pickups. I kicked the bike into neutral and coasted down the approach and quietly right up to the campfire two men were tending. A five-year old boy rode up on a small quad, skidded to a stop, then kind of sneered at my bike and asked what kind it was. Showing me how unimpressed he was and who had the real power at this point, he kicked the little bike into gear and spun off across the muddy flat. After a short exchange of greetings, the fellows gave me a gallon of gas in exchange for one of my books, and I was good to go.

Later I discovered that there is no better way to meet people than parking your bike just outside the window and walking into a restaurant in dripping wet leathers. I met several people this way in Grande Cache, Hinton, Jasper, Blue River, Barrier and Kamloops. In each place, several folks were more than generous with their advice, which ranged from "get yourself some handle grip warmers and a pair of elephant ears, young fellow," to "I think you are rushing the season. You should stay home another month."

Deep down I sensed they all really wished they were riding with me, as there is a certain feeling of satisfaction and excitement in being the only bike on the highway. I felt like the Lone Ranger as I pulled up my face bandana and rode off with a wave as they turned to each other and said, "Who was that masked idiot?"

I stopped at home in Kelowna for the night, planning to continue the last leg Saturday, but in the morning when I pulled in the clutch handle, it broke off and I was not going anywhere. It seems I clipped it when parking the bike the night before. I visited the local Suzuki dealer, but he did not have a handle in stock and thought it would take a week to get one.

The Vernon store had closed for the holiday, so I tried the Yamaha dealership. They were true bike enthusiasts; more concerned about getting me on the road than the fact that I was not riding one of their models, but unable to produce a handle, they sold me a membership to the Star Touring and Riding Association instead. Here I was stuck with less than an hour of riding left to reach Slack Alice's in Penticton it would be an understatement to say I was disappointed.

I began doing what I do best, pout, when the wife came to my rescue by calling the parts department at S & V Motorcycle World Ltd. in Vancouver. Not only did Brian Silderman have the part, he agreed to run it over to the bus after work so I would have it Easter Sunday, providing the freight depot was open. Then he began asking every customer that day if by chance they were going to Kelowna. Late in the afternoon, he called back to say Joe Goetz, a fellow from Westbank, had just been in his store and agreed to bring the lever to me the same night. Talk about brother bikers going the extra mile to look out for one another. Sunday morning I was on the road again.

It may not have been easy to get to Slack Alice's, but I made it. It was a great show and shine. There was plenty to see, from beautiful old bikes to the latest custom choppers, and best of all – warm sunshine. I suggest you add this event to your list of places you must ride to before you die.

෴

*Leaders do things for people without expecting a reward,*
*yet greater rewards do follow them.*
*Leaders never focus on what did not go the way they expected but make the most of what is. Because of this event I joined the Star group and it was Star members who came my rescue a few years later in Reno.*
*All thanks to a broken clutch leaver.*

# 11. Riding the Rockies in April

"Why don't you swing by Calgary and drop me off on your way to Grande Prairie?" said the wife, obviously never having added up the mileage, as it is 400- kilometers farther than going direct.

But when a wife offers to crawl on the back of a bike for her first 600-kilometer trip, it is best to take advantage of the situation, so we loaded up and left the sunny Okanagan early on the last Sunday of April.

She did not have cool biking gear, so she wore her skiing outfit. A third of the way into the trip, I slowed down in order to reduce the wind-chill, wishing I had a heated vest. The wife was chatting with excitement, telling me how wonderful the mountains, trees and ditch looked cloaked in a fresh dusting of snow. Then she thanked me for taking it a little slower so she could enjoy all there is too see.

I quietly shivered through lunch and wished I had handle-grip warmers, but hey, it was still above freezing, and the wife was still smiling and commenting how much more she had seen on this trip than any of the hundreds we had made over this same road by car.

It's impossible to ride through the Canadian Rockies without seeing wildlife and it's exhilarating to see an elk close up as it leaps onto the road from the ditch. I didn't know elk could run that fast. I've had deer try to commit suicide by leaping in front of me, I've had moose gallop onto the road and challenge me, I've even had two grizzlies lay on the road and just look at me like dinner had just arrived, but elk usually keep on grazing oblivious to everything. This one however, thought it might be fun to scare the hell out of me. The wife thought the elk was cute, bouncing alongside the bike.

She continued to smile as we passed through Banff, unaware that small parts of me had become frozen and I longed for a heated seat. She said she didn't want to stop as she was enjoying the trip, so I had to swallow my pride and admit that I had to stop before the frozen parts fell off and rolled down the highway.

"F-F-Finally we are in Ca-Ca-Ca-Calgary." It is hard to sound macho when stuttering three octaves higher through the icicles that dangle from the moustache. The wife gave me a hug as we walked into the hotel and said she so

*Col. Layton Park*

enjoyed the trip that she would help me warm up. True to her word, she drew me a nice warm bath, and then turned in.

***Leaders always ask these three important questions***:
1. ***What did we do right***, *what could we have done better and what did we learn?*
   So what did I do right? Agreeing to take the wife on a ride is always the right thing to do. She loved the adventure and has enjoyed biking even more in warm weather.
2. ***What could I have done better?*** *I should have taken the time to ensure we had the right, warm, equipment for the mountains. This is especially true in the shoulder seasons. Do you think through your equipment requirements before each adventure? Good pilots always use a checklist.*
3. ***What did I learn?*** *It is better to feel warm than to look cool.*
   I am prepared the next time we decide to ride from Spokane to Billings and the wife says, "Why don't we swing by Chicago on the way?"

*K1200LT BMW in Grande Cache snow*

# 12. Code of the Road

*The code of the road ain't some words on a page*
*It's something you know, when you come of age*
*The code guarantees all honor their word*
*What happens on the road should never be heard*
   *(Apologies to Roger Miller)*

The code of the road is an age-old unspoken contract between travelers that says what happens on the road stays on the road. When some people are away from their hometowns, commitments and obligations, or at war or on an adventure, and are far away from all who know them, they indulge in indiscretion. Those traveling with them accept this unspoken contract guaranteeing their privacy. A guarantee forever honored by all those who venture out on the road.

    This is a commitment that I take seriously, but … I am also a writer, and the fellows I traveled with should have known better than to include a writer in their road adventures. Sorry, guys, but I have no filters. The good news is no one I know reads much of what I write, so this unabridged secret of our trip should be safe.

    Some may think that four non-drinking guys north of fifty would not have much fun or get carried away while on the road… but *aw contraire*.

    We were only in Kentucky two days when one of my fellow travelers came back to the room telling us with excitement that we had to see what he'd stumbled on while exploring the hotel.

    This was our most conservative member, a fellow who is happily married and would not do anything to jeopardize the strong relationship he has with his wife, yet already the road was seducing his values.

    "Are you sure we should be doing this?" Bob asked.

    "For sure we should! I'm not passing up the most beautiful thing I have ever seen," answered Denny.

    "I don't know," Bob, stuttered, "Tell us again what she said."

    "She made an offer you wouldn't believe. She said I could have anything I wanted, and when I told her about you guys, she said you could come too."

"But what if someone finds out?" Hoss asked.

"Who is going to find out? I looked around, there is no one here who knows us, and none of us will tell. You know the code and all." Denny was almost bouncing as he spoke.

"But if my wife found out, she would – " Hoss was interrupted by Denny.

"Come on," he said. "If any of our wives find out, we'll all be in big trouble, but they won't. We will stick together on this, right?" He sounded so sure you could see the others beginning to give in.

"Guys, this is a once-in-a-lifetime road trip. A time to forget who we are and taste the forbidden fruits. I'm going. Are you coming or not?"

Denny's enthusiasm was becoming infectious. As he headed out the door, the three of us followed closely behind.

For the next four days, our mornings began the same way. As soon as we had showered, we rushed down to see the woman, who welcomed us warmly and true to her word, let us have all we wanted.

Without a doubt, she was in charge of the best buffet I had ever seen. Southern biscuits smothered in thick gravy topped with fresh peaches or oranges and a side plate piled high with crisp bacon. The spread was unbelievable, and the side dishes of fruit-filled crepes and new pastries were incredible. Even now, I get teary-eyed just thinking about it.

"So this is what it has come to," Denny said one morning. "This is considered walking on the wild side, eating all the things we shouldn't, and afraid that our wives might find out?

"Afraid our doctors will hear we did not follow their advice. Afraid they will know we did not follow the Canadian Food Guide.

"Whatever happened to wine, women and song? What will be next, racing wheelchairs recklessly down the halls of the senior's homes?"

Time levels all things, yet sometimes I still catch myself dreaming of that thick gravy. My wife suspects something when she sees my smile, but I will not weaken and tell her.

I know I shouldn't have told you either as you were not there with us, but can you imagine that you were accept the code-of-the-road, and not mention it to anyone?

༄

***A leader stands by his friends and associates.***

# 13. Canadian Military Secret Revealed!

News Break! Tim Horton's is secretly working for the Canadian Military! Suspicion was raised when Tim Horton's announced they were opening an outlet in Afghanistan and looking for people who can serve donuts, make chili and pour coffee with one hand while disarming Taliban guerillas and fire a machine gun with the other. A ban was immediately placed on the soldiers to keep them from applying for the higher-paying positions.

My sources tell me it was the U.S. military who insisted Tim Horton's be brought in to calm the Canadian soldiers who were becoming too aggressive without their morning double-double.

Canada has been accused of using unnecessary force, as happened when one soldier single-handedly took down a dozen guerilla fighters using only a coffee spoon. When interviewed, the solider said it was a terrible misunderstanding as he had mistaken them for Tim Horton employees and was only trying to get their attention. The Canadian Government offered apologies to terrorists everywhere and issued each of the fighters twenty thousand Canadian Tire dollars in compensation.

In a related story, the Canadian Government is rumored to have contracted with Tim's to act as our first line of defense should the country be attacked. The plan is if Canada is invaded, all the Tim Horton's will immediately close. Experts speculate that by noon the Canadian public will become so hyper and angry without its morning fix that they will rise up and strike down any invading force. This came about as the result of a blind test study in which a Tim Horton's, located beside a seniors home, substituted its coffee with a no-name brand. Two elderly ladies who coffee there every morning became so agitated that they kicked the crap out of two passing Hell's Angels, stole their bikes and rode across town to get a cup from another location.

A Spokesman for Hell's Angels says it proves nothing – their members are only gentlemen motorcycle enthusiasts and one of the women was armed with a walking stick. A spokesman for the Royal Canadian Mounted Police, who were conducting training exercises inside the location at the time, said he did not witness the takedown as they were stuck in the donut lineup.

The military refused to comment, and a spokesman for Tim Horton's just smiled and in a tinny voice said, "Will that be all?"

In researching the story, I asked a professor who studies the effect of stimulants on the brain at the University of British Columbia's Faculty of Arts, why Tim's coffee seems to have such an overpowering effect on regular users. He took a long drag from a funny-smelling cigarette, sipped a Starbucks coffee, and said, "Whatever."

When I pressed him for an answer, he said he believes there is a conspiracy going on, as Tim Horton's is a giant right-wing, for-profit Eastern Canadian conglomerate. In the lower mainland (or as it is known in the rest of the province, the Land beyond Hope), people prefer Starbuck's. He said they believe Starbucks is a socially conscious non-profit organization that promotes peace throughout the world by offering Columbian products at reasonable prices.

He refused to comment further as he has a grant to study coffee for the next four years and will release a paper at that time. In the meantime, a reporter for the *Calgary Herald* reported seeing Prime Minister Steve sipping on a Tim's and eating a double-glazed maple at the Stampede.

I hesitated to break this story in the interest of national security, but decided it doesn't matter if this story falls into the hands of alien forces, as they will not understand the power Tim's is capable of wielding. This is demonstrated by the American belief that Crispy Cream is somehow capable of overthrowing Tim's and dominating Canada, but fear not our leaders and defense experts say that the combined power of the Canadian Military and Tim Horton's is unstoppable, so you can sleep soundly tonight. That is if you haven't drunk any of Tim's coffee in the past couple of hours.

༄

***I dedicate this story to our armed forces, which provide us leadership in defense of our country and life style.***
***The next time you see a member of one of our forces in line at a Timmies, step up and pay for their coffee.***
***That is the least we can do.***

# 14. Spring Run-Off

I look forward to The Okanagan Spring Run-Off. It is the first ride of the season, with over a hundred bikes participating in a ride from Kelowna, B.C. up the west side of Okanagan Lake to the city of Vernon, returning along the west side of Kalamalka and Woods Lake.

The local RCMP were on hand to assist the bikes out of the parking lot after they checked to make sure that license plates were bolted on properly and other potential hazards were properly taken care of. Every type of bike imaginable was present – sport, dual sport, cruisers, touring bikes, old bikes, new bikes and not-so-sure-what-the-heck-they-were bikes.

The collection of riders was even more varied, from one young man with a learner's sticker on his back, to old people like Bill Hubbard, owner of Century 21 Executives in Vernon. (He pointed out that he may be old, but he is still ten years younger than I am.) I told him if he rode his Gold Wing alongside of me, he might end up in a column revealing to the world how he ploughed his first bike into a van and lived to tell the story. If you are ever in Vernon, ask him to give you the safety pointers he learned from that event. But I digress.

The run began in Kelowna and thundered around, up and down the west-side road, which must have been built especially for motorcycles. There is nothing more spectacular than bikes strung out on a road with so many turns that sometimes you can see the back of your own helmet. Of course, having beautiful tree-covered hills to your left – no, wait. Don't look at the hills because the ditch on the right is 800 feet straight down into the Okanagan Lake. Not only is the feeling of riding a road that has turns in it exciting for this prairie boy, but having warm sunshine in late April is a treat as well.

The ride included a lunch stop in Vernon with a buffet that contained more choices that even I could eat. After we waddled back out to our bikes, we continued on to Kelowna for final prize draws.

The entire event (including a tee-shirt, lunch and prizes) was only $25, most of which wound up as a donation to the local General Hospital to fund neat stuff for bad motorcycle drivers. (You don't have to write in… we know who you are.)

*Col. Layton Park*

*∽*

***Funny, I wrote this before I was one of those injured motorcyclists… I guess I should have been kinder.***

**Sage Advice by Woody:**

*Eighty percent of success is showing up.*

*Money is better than poverty, if only for financial reasons.*

*You can live to be a hundred if you give up all the things that make you want to live to be a hundred.*

*The talent for being happy is appreciating and liking what you have, instead of what you do not have.*

Quotes by: Woody Allen born: 1935-12-01

# 15. Don't Park —Wright

I was excited that Ed Wright, an old biking buddy from years ago, visited me on his new Harley Road King. The two black-and-chrome bikes looked great together, and we were itching to ride.

I wanted to impress Ed with the beauty of riding in the Okanagan, so I took him to Lake Country on the old highway that winds between Kelowna and Winfield, then over the high country between the valleys, separating The Woods Lake chain from Lake Okanagan. We wound down a small, tight, paved road so full of switchbacks it would make a rattler dizzy. Arriving at Okanagan Center we stopped for an ice cream cone and drank in the view of people playing in the water.

We enjoyed the warm sun before zipping up our leather jackets and continuing on. Ed suggested we should wear our chaps, but it was a hot day and I pointed out that I had not dropped my bike in forty years, so I told him I could risk one afternoon of easy riding.

Leaving Okanagan Centre, we climbed almost straight up through the fields of grapevines to visit the Grey Monk Estate Winery, which juts out from the side of the hill. After standing on the deck overlooking the beautiful lake, we make dinner reservations for the following evening. The lot is so steep that the winery has two tiers for parking. To exit, we had to go up a sharp incline to the higher tier. I was almost at the top and still had not heard the roar of the Road King, so I looked back. In doing so, I backed off the throttle enough that my bike stalled. I pulled in the clutch and brake levers, then as I put out my left leg, discovered a bit of an optical illusion where the roadway slopes down considerably to the left.

I have a thirty-three inch inseam, but that was about a foot too short, and my foot kept going down without contacting the ground. I felt the heavy bike begin to lean past the balancing point and knew it was about to go over. I decided it was time to bail and drop my bike. As I was flying through the air, I was wishing I hadn't mentioned the bit about not dropping my bike in forty years.

There is no graceful way to dive, hit the pavement, and complete a couple of rolls, then finish with a spread eagle in front of the dozen or so people who are watching. If they all had score-cards, I'm sure I would have looked up to a row of 4's and 5's at best. I was trying to get to my feet while some well-intentioned wannabe paramedic rushed over and put a hand firmly on my back, hollering, "Stay down, you might be hurt." I was hurt all right. My knees were missing skin and bleeding, but that didn't compare to the pain my ego was feeling. Several other fellows rushed to my aid as a crowd began to gather. I became the center of attention for everyone in the area. Meanwhile Ed's bike roared to life, and he quickly rode up beside me to ensure I was not badly hurt.

I can now confirm that the only thing funnier than seeing a big leather-jacketed biker fall off his bike, facedown in a parking lot, is to see two bikers fall facedown in a parking lot. And that is exactly what happened, when Ed stopped and tried to put out his leg, with its much smaller inseam, down. The two big black-and-chrome bikes may have looked great standing together in our driveway, but when they were lying side by side on the ground with both riders spread out next to them – well, we weren't doing the tough biker image a whole lot of good.

I asked him if he had to copy everything I do and as he lay there in the gravel, he looked at me and smiled simply saying, "Yes you are my hero."

In my mind, I could hear someone say, "They just don't Park-Wright."

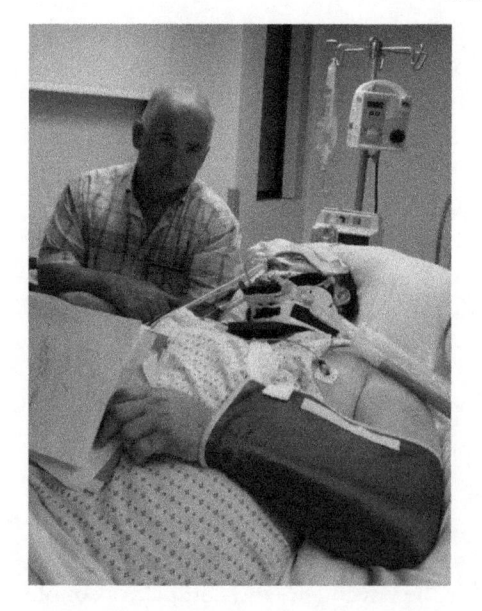

୬

*A side note, when I woke up in Reno, it was Ed Wright who was standing next to the bed so now he is my hero!*

*Ed tried again, to copy my stunt, by driving off the highway just a month after my accident but he failed to even break skin.*

*I am not sure what leadership principles are at play here, but Ed has had a very successful career as a leader in the oil industry and perhaps it is his willingness to stroke other people's ego, such as calling them his hero, may be why he is so well liked and admired.*

**Good leaders let the light shine on those around them.**

# 16. Motivating Teenagers

I grew up in a small prairie town that was nine miles from a lake. Every good-looking girl lived out of town on a farm, and it was cold for ten months of the year with no warm malls to hang out in. So every young man needed a car or a motorcycle.

The only sport we had was "flipping U-ees on Main." Flipping U-ees consisted of spending the evening driving the full length of Main Street, revving the bike, waving at the girls, trying to talk them into getting on the back, then doing a U-turn and doing it again.

You could wave at the same girls a lot in three hours because Main Street was only two blocks long.

As a result, every fifteen-year-old was motivated to work. As soon as we had saved two or three hundred dollars, we would buy a motorbike. Four hundred dollars, if we decided to buy insurance and plates for it, although that seemed to be an optional then.

The wife also worked from an early age, so she cannot understand why our sixteen-year old son isn't motivated to find a job.

"Well honey, let's review his life. He lives six blocks from one of the best beaches in Canada where he can hang out with bikini-clad girls. They all wave at the guys with motorcycles and cars, but they only cruise back and forth looking for a place to park, or are stuck in traffic and not going anywhere. Taking a ride to the beach these days is a liability, not an asset."

Our son isn't motivated by want of a wardrobe, as the entire group of young people he hangs out with doesn't use a full change of clothes between them. They wear the same bathing suits every day and spend all their time in the water or on the beach where there isn't anything to spend money on.

The girls all live within walking distance of our house or on a bus route, so there is no need for wheels. In fact, the only time he needed a ride in the past two years was when he and a friend got caught at the beach in a downpour. Believe it or not, they jogged over to the local pizza place, ordered a pizza to be delivered to our house, and then asked the driver if they could ride home with him.

"It was cheaper than a taxi, and we all got something to eat." He explained, especially cheap because he had me dish out for the pizza. You have to give them full marks for creativity, so how do you motivate teenagers growing up in Utopia?

I had purchased an older Honda 250 that I let him drive so he could run some errands for us, and when it broke down, the wife suggested he get a job to pay for the repairs. He decided he didn't really need the Honda, so it sat until the wife realized that she was the one being punished because she could no longer send him on errands.

Recently I spoke to a group and began by saying that I used to have five theories on how to raise perfect children, but now I have five children and no theories. At the break, a woman introduced herself as a psychologist and wanted to hear more about my four theories.

Seems that I don't understand my children and my audiences don't understand my jokes. Am I slipping?

I was lamenting these problems to my buddy Ditch, who laughed and said, "Your son hangs out at the beach where he can watch scantily dressed girls, the weather is always nice, he can go home to a nice house and eat well, he plays a number of sports, but he doesn't work. Is that the problem?"

"Yes, that is the problem," I answered.

"If that was you, what would it take to motivate *you* to look for a job?" Ditch asked.

Then I realized: my son is living my dream for moving here in the first place! It disturbs me that the kids got a forty-year head start.

☙

*Both sons have since graduated and are doing well. Liam, the younger, decided to hitch hike across Canada and when asked if he wasn't a little nervous said, "Of course I am nervous, I have never jumped into the universe before!"*
*When was the last time you jumped into the universe? Leaders are always pushing their envelope or comfort zone.*

# 17. Motorcycle Airbags?

The news article said "a woman spilled her full-size cruiser but she was saved when her breast implants acted like an air bag, saving her from extensive injury." She probably regretted not opting for the Botox lip and nose job as well. If she had, she could have made a perfect three-point landing and all injuries would have been avoided.

I understand that several government officials have already volunteered to look into the advantages of implants to decide if every female rider should be required to get them and what would be the perfect size. Pamela Anderson was hired as an expert on the subject and asked if she had ever fallen and had her implants save her from injury. She reported that, hard as it is to believe, she has never fallen forward.

The paper also reported that the woman's boyfriend, who was riding on the back, suffered sever road rash to the backs of his hands. Once again demonstrating the need to wear protective gloves on your hands or hold onto something safer when riding. Perhaps that is what caused the woman to lose control, and next time perhaps he should keep a bag of Jell-O in each pocket to play with instead.

In an unrelated story, Sumo-wrestlers were reported getting implants on the top of their head so they could meet minimum height requirements for their sport. (No kidding. I could not make this stuff up.)

This got me to thinking there is a whole new industry just waiting to happen. If we could get implants approved as safety equipment, we could do away with helmets. Finally, a lot of large-headed riders could be free of the uncomfortable and overheated brain buckets.

Riders could shed their heavy leathers for tank tops during the hot days of summer… providing they didn't mind being a little busty. A side effect for guys is other guys might think twice about hitting them in a barroom brawl, giving them that split-second advantage that often makes the difference. Depending on the size of their cleavage and how heavy their beard is, they might not even have to buy their own drinks.

As the days become cooler again, I find it easier to wear all my gear, but how far do we have to go? Did the leathers and helmets help the Montreal rider who had an overpass fall on him? Were the folks in the cars beside him any better off? The only way to remain perfectly safe is not to leave the house and hope an airplane doesn't fall on it while you are home.

I'm reminded of the big push for ski helmets a few years ago when Sonny Bono died less than a week after Michael, the 39-year-old son of Robert F. Kennedy, who also died skiing. It seems whenever there is a sensational accident or celebrity death we all have to pay a higher price somehow.

I couldn't help but think what would happen if someone famous got carried away and died after striking the headboard too hard?

The official in charge of Homeland and Sexual Protection (HASP) would propose a law that everyone has to wear a helmet while having sex. I can hear the wife now… "Not tonight, honey. I can't find my helmet." Or she feels in the mood during the wee morning hours, and I turn her down because I left the helmet on the handlebars of the bike in the garage. After all, none of us wants to do anything illegal.

So where is this all going, you ask? Frankly, this meandering was my way of getting my mind off that poor lady sliding down the road on her air bags. I had begun to think of what kind of first aid you should offer to apply to such an accident victim, mouth to mouth? Then I decided I should occupy my mind with more meaningful thoughts. That's when I remembered there are opportunities in every situation and the business possibilities started to come to me.

So, watch for my new implant protection system, which will be marketed under the name "Tough Inner Trauma Shields" or by its acronym T.I.T.S. for short.

If you think it is something you would like to buy to protect a woman you care for, call me. I'll drop by and measure her for the equipment myself.

ɞ

*Warning I can find no valuable leadership principles in this piece it is the pure ramblings of a biker who started riding before the helmet laws. If you can find something relative, let me know.*

# 18. If You Had to Pick a Bike as a Mate

If you had to pick a motorcycle as a mate, which one would you choose? Someone asked the question the other night, and it raised a number of interesting thoughts.

One woman suggested that she'd like to spend her life with an Italian crotch rocket... sleek and fast, hugging her curves tightly. Perhaps too tightly, I suggested. How will you keep it satisfied running up and down the same old road? What happens when it begins to look for a more challenging road or feels there are getting to be too many frost heaves and starts to look for a smoother surface?

"No," I said. I don't think most women would be happy married to a crotch rocket, to which an Italian woman replied that she thinks they are overrated. She said they only perform well if you keep them revved high. She said they are quick to shift, which is fun at first, but too much work over the long haul.

Another woman suggested she would want to spend her life with a new Gold Wing... "You know, the one that has enough compartments to carry all my luggage, shoes and a week's groceries, yet still outperforms that Italian bike."

A fourth woman said she wanted the bike with the largest V-twin made. "Just the thought of that big power plant throbbing as it idles in my driveway excites me," she observed, adding that the color should be red, because that also excites her.

I wondered if she would still be happy when the shine fades and the bike becomes hard to keep tuned, leaving it performing poorly and consuming more fuel than anything else in the neighborhood.

This is hard. Think about it. Which bike would you choose?

The last woman's husband felt a large motocross machine was the right answer. He said that big bulky cruisers are too hard to handle. He likes to be able to get down and dirty, and no matter how deep the ruts, they just want to keep going. They are also handy to have around the house because they can pack a ton of stuff, don't consume a lot of fuel and are just fun to be with.

Another fellow suggested a Harley Sportster was the only way to go, at which a fellow rider started to laugh, saying he had a wife like that. "Sure she was sleek and good to look at, but she didn't always work and he got tired of how loud she was."

I said I thought my wife would choose a full dresser. I'm not speaking about a wimpy, shiny BMW. I mean the biggest, squarest, heaviest bike on the road. It too consumes a lot but goes anywhere. It doesn't pretend to be sleek or fancy yet stands out in a crowd. It's easy to love even though most women feel it's completely impractical. Best of all, they don't wear out and will perform for years. At least that's what I choose to believe. *(It should be noted that after writing this article I bought a BMW K1200 LS)* When the wife heard my comment, she laughed and suggested that she might be compelled to choose a scooter. She doesn't care that they are small, and she likes the idea that they're built for one. They're not the fastest and don't have a big power plant, but they are very efficient, turn on a dime, and are cute in a funny sort of way.

Me, a scooter? I don't think so. Do you think she is sending me a message or just messing with my mind? The thought of it makes my hair hurt. I am beginning to think this mate-as-a-bike was one of the dumbest questions I've ever been asked.

# 19. How to Tell a Real Biker…

It is good to see the growing number of bikes on the road these days, but if you are one of the new riders, I want to point out the clues that betray your attempts to portray yourself as a seasoned biker.

One of the most important habits to develop is learning to chew before you spit out bugs that fly in your mouth.

Don't spend more time shining your bike than riding it, and never admit you haven't driven down a gravel road.

Don't grab a hairbrush as soon as you take your helmet off or carry a laptop in the saddlebags.

Begin riding to work in order to create wrinkles and creases in your leathers they should look worn and not all match.

Never admit you own a rain suit or ride by store windows to admire your reflection.

As a new rider, you will find seasoned bikers welcome you, if you actually ride your bike and your average trip does not consist of riding across town to Timmy's for bike night.

Don't worry about the year or make of your bike. Real bikers ride old bikes and new. They ride Harleys, English, Japanese and other foreign or domestic-made bikes. They ride chopped bikes and stock bikes, big bikes and small bikes. The commonality among all these is the word "ride." So start today and extend the community in a way that benefits us all.

There seems to be a current police crackdown on bikers, and I think it is getting a little out of hand. The other day I parked my Boulevard and went into Tim Horton's to grab a quick coffee. When I came out, there was a cop writing a parking ticket, so I went up to him and said, "Come on, sir, how about giving a guy a break?"

The cop ignored me and continued writing the ticket, so I called him a jerk. He looked over my leathers, sneered at me then started writing another ticket for worn and unsafe tires, so I said I thought he was an ass.

He finished the second ticket and struck it between the bars and the windshield with the first ticket. I laughed at him and said, "That was a big job for you. Maybe you should go in for another donut and take a break."

*Col. Layton Park*

He began to get red under the collar and started writing a third ticket. So I made a reference about his mother running out from under the front step and biting him when he gets home, so he started writing a fourth. This continued for some time, as I kept giving abuse and he found more and more reasons to write tickets.

Finally, I had enough, so I turned and walked away, leaving him angrily writing. As I rounded the corner, I said to another rider I was with, "I never did like the Harley driver that owns the bike over there by that cop, and I bet he is going to be pissed." Then I mounted my own bike and rode away.

Okay, so that is not a true story, nor is it a good way to build relationships with The Man, but don't you know someone that you would actually like to do that to?

❧

**The only good leadership point I can think of in this story is know when to keep your mouth shut, no matter how tempting.**
*Take the other day for example.*

*I stopped into the local A&W for coffee and an older man began asking questions about my ride. He said he had retired here over 25 years ago. I said, "You must have taken an early retirement, what did you do?"*

*He sat up straight and with a look of importance said in an arrogant tone, "I was the Senior VP of nine companies."*
*Following good leadership traits I smiled rather than voicing what I wanted to say, "Too bad, you were so close to making it to the top. Are you bitter?"*

# 20. *My Obituary*

The trouble with being over sixty is the only social events I seem to attend are funerals. Recently I met an old friend, John Abbot-Brown at one and he said he visits the funeral home every Saturday for the free sandwiches. Even if he doesn't know the deceased, he said he sees someone he knows.

We talked about how standard funerals are a church service for someone who did not attend church. The grandchildren read bible passages and everyone cries, unlike my father's funeral, where the grandchildren told funny stories about their grandpa in a celebration of his life and everyone laughed. That's what I want... laughter.

I've decided I should not trust it to those I leave behind to give me a fun send-off so I have written my own obituary. I know it will not be used for many more years, in fact, I intend to outlive most of you, and longer than Duke, (See the following story about Duke) so this is your chance to hear it. I wrote this just prior to the accident when I almost needed it. Somehow it is just not as funny now but here it is anyway.

*We are born alone and we die alone, so between those times we should enjoy those we travel with along the road of life...* nah... true but a little too sucky. How about, *"I was born in bed with a woman I love and hopefully will pass the same way?"* Kinda catchy.

I enjoyed great relationships with my parents, Robert and Dorothy, as well as with their parents. My sisters and their husbands and I are blessed with too many wonderful nieces, nephews and funny, funny cousins, to mention.

Those who walked life's path closest to me were my daughters Katherine, Shauna and my chosen daughter, (niece) Jeannine and their families, which I expect to be huge by the time this is required.

My sons Carson and Liam refused to walk with me, they always wanted to run which helped to keep me young and panting although Myrna thinks all the panting was because of her. By the time, this is required, I expect there to be other in-laws as well as dozens of grandchildren, but surely someone can fill in those names, as I choose not to dwell on this subject again.

The person who walked or ran by my side, laughed and cried with me, my dearest friend, confidant, business partner and wife, Myrna, gave me unconditional love, and for that I will always be eternally grateful.

## Col. Layton Park

They say that marriage is like a game of cards where you start with a couple of hearts and a diamond, then end up looking for club and a spade. Myrna still discards the clubs… so far so good.

Those of us who find true soul mates are truly wealthy-just don't let her plan the thing. In my case, Myrna intends to give out the final summary sheets (I am sure they have a better name but it escapes me right now) in sheet protectors, a favorite item for me. On top of that, she says that those small sandwiches will be served from the dozens of the small storage containers I can't resist buying at every Rubbermaid sale.

She hasn't said but I think she plans on letting you take them home after the slide show. Oh that is the next thing I have to do, build a slide show so I can have one last laugh at everyone else's expense.

I wanted my buddies to form a missing man formation fly-by but realized all those coots will be too old to be let near an airplane so I will opt for the pegs down procession if any of them can still swing a leg over a bike.

☙

***I wrote this morbid piece before being inspired by Duke Proctor and my accident which made we realize that I should be thinking about living, not dying.***

*My bike in northern Nevada and my ambulance in the background.*

# 21. Duke Proctor Dead at 106

I never knew Duke, but I liked him anyway. How can you not admire a man who makes the national news on more than one occasion? A man so honored, not for his financial accomplishments, not for winning trophies, not for being a hero, although he was one, but for being the man next door who was a leader by demonstrating to everyone how we should live life.

My sister "DS," the Lumby Realtor who likes to remain anonymous, and who I like to publically tease because I think she is so great, tells me Duke had a great sense of humour. He always walked erect*, drove his car and lived on his own for years after he turned one hundred years old.

Duke square-danced weekly until he was 103, continued to play horseshoes until he was 104, and while I still struggled to reach a bowling score of 105, he was bowling regularly at age 105.

I was less than half Duke's age when I first began to complain about feeling old. I felt my body was letting me down. Then I would read about Duke doing something that I thought I was too old to do, and it would inspire me.

Mind you, my mind played tricks and I would sometimes think, "If he can do that at a hundred, why get in shape now? I can put it off another twenty years then still do what he does at that age." (Save the paper: don't write and tell me I'm crazy. My family is way ahead of you on that one.)

While many of us sat home thinking the Armistice Day Parade is a little too long to walk on a chilly day, Duke was out there every year until his last, leading the parade then standing at attention throughout the service in honour of the boys he served with that did not come back. He did not forget, and in the end he was the oldest of only four surviving Canadian First World War veterans.

I was feeling nervous about standing on a chair because it seemed too high, when the National News announced that Duke had celebrated his one-hundredth birthday by skydiving. I am nervous about jumping to conclusions, and here he is jumping out of an airplane. These were not the actions of some eccentric old man. This was a man who just kept on living life to the fullest.

*Col. Layton Park*

When Duke was young (in his early sixties), he lived in Squaw Valley on the Mabel Lake Road. He hired two teenage boys from the area, Gerald Clowry and his brother Ron. They worked at the bottom loading the elevator with bales while Duke, at the top, took them off and stacked them in the loft. The younger brothers thought it would be funny to wear the old boy down, so they piled bales on as fast as they could, giggling at the thought that soon he would tell them to take a break.

Gerald and Ron were ready to drop when they stopped for lunch. Gerald took off his hat, wiped his brow, and as he looked up through the sweat he saw Duke slide down the rails of the elevator. Duke smiled at them and said, "Good work, boys. If we keep this pace up, we will be done by supper."

According to Gerald, Duke often said, "Let's see if we can crowd two days' work into one." In the end, this gentleman crowded two lifetimes into one.

*Darline says she doesn't not know this for sure....*

*I don't know if Duke ever rode a bike but I wanted to thank him for the inspiration and his leadership by example.*

**Happiness is your dentist telling you it won't hurt and then having him catch his hand in the drill.** (Apology to Dr. Jack DeGruchy)

**Johnny Carson**

## 22. The Back Inversion Machine

I was struggling with back problems, so the wife took me shopping for a gravity inversion system. It is easy to use, just set it for your height, strap your ankles in, then allow yourself to fall backwards until your feet are straight up and your head is straight down and the weight of your own body stretches out the back. It seemed to feel good at the store, so we bought one. Then I set it up in a room in the basement of our store, where I stay when I am in Grande Prairie.

When I was finished putting it together, I took a shower and thought I might try it out before I got ready for bed. What I did not know is the height setting is just a guide as everyone's center of gravity is different depending on how your weight is distributed. The other thing I was unaware of is that the center of gravity shifts upward (toward your head) as you turn over, and everything slides in that direction. The machine flipped me upside-down very easily.

The blood rushed to my head, not wanting to stay upside-down too long I attempted to flip myself back up. Unfortunately, my center of gravity had shifted too far toward the ground, and I could not make the machine flip back. I tried again with no luck. I was beginning to panic a little as I hung upside-down naked with all the blood rushing to my brain, still unable to turn right-side up. I was beginning to picture how it would look in the morning when the sales staff arrived at the store finding me dead, naked and hanging like a side of beef.

Then I saw my cell phone lying on the edge of my bed. It was within reach, but I didn't know who to call. I could call 911, but I began to ask myself which was worse, the staff finding me dead like this or the paramedics finding me still alive but in the same naked upside-down condition. At least dead, I wouldn't have to live with the fallout, but alive, well, this is a small town, and the story would get out. How would I explain it to people? Maybe dieing was the best alternative.

I had been using the phone and the phone book just prior to taking the shower, and I could reach the book, so I decided to call a close friend who would not tell. Then I realized I do not have any friends who could keep that kind of secret. On the other hand, I do have one friend, Dennis, who embellishes stories so much no one believes him anyway, so I thought perhaps I should call him. I grabbed the book and tried to look up his number while hanging upside-down, the blood pressure behind my eyes making it hard to read the numbers.

Wait – I cannot call Dennis, I thought, even if no one believes him the story will still be all over town. Frustrated, I put the phone on my lap, but the weight of the book, my hands and the cell phone changed the center of gravity again, slowly at first then as everything shifted downward suddenly the table flew upward at a high rate of speed. I was a little too dizzy from the time spent upside-down to anticipate the sudden stop it was about to make as the footboard came in contact with the floor and launched me forward like a missile. Fortunately, my ankles were still strapped in, so instead of flying forward, only the upper part of my body did while my feet stayed firmly grounded on the unit.

I noticed when I picked myself up off the floor, that although I had several more aches and pains than I started with, my back did feel a little better.

I have now mastered the inversion machine however when you begin using it perhaps it is best to also use a spotter.

☙

***A good leader will bend over backwards to get a job done… : ) Okay it's lame but it is also late and I am running out of leadership examples for some of these stories.***

*Glory is fleeting, but obscurity is forever.*

*Never interrupt your enemy when he is making a mistake.*

*History is the version of past events that people have decided to agree upon.*

*In politics, an absurdity is not a handicap.*

*Religion is what keeps the poor from murdering the rich.*
                         Napoleon Bonaparte born: 1769-08-15 - died: 1821-05-05

## 23. Surprises Kill the Elderly

I got a note from a reader who suggested that I warn my readers not to give surprises to seniors as many are on heart medication, other pharmaceuticals, or are taking Viagra and this added excitement could cause blood pressure to rise dramatically, resulting in tragedy.

"A big surprise can cause death," he warned, saying that he knew of five cases where surprise parties had negative endings. I appreciated his concern and am passing his warning along.

Meanwhile, I have been thinking about how to put this serious warning into a humour column, but I think there is a rule that states, *no joking about croaking*. I just couldn't make it work humorously, so here it is straight up (no offence to the Viagra users).

The wife loves to give me surprise presents, and although I am not quite a senior and only use Viagra on hot summer nights to keep the warm sheets off my legs, she should be more careful. I would just die some Christmas morning if I found a new motorcycle under the tree.

A riding buddy said I am going to die anyway because she hinted she wanted something clear and set in silver, and I intend to surprise her with a new windshield for her Bergman. He doesn't think the wife will appreciate that. Still I hope she likes it better than the riding leathers she asked for a few years ago, even if she didn't mean leather-fringed underwear.

In the past, the wife has given me a West Coast kayak trip, a weekend alone in L.A. as well as other adventure trips. Recently she sent me to a stand-up comedy course in Vancouver. For a week we learned the secrets of writing jokes, worked on developing my own material, and then spent two days in class polishing the set. Graduation consisted of presenting at the Laughing Bean Coffee house on Hastings. I told the story of the bike reunion and got a great response.

My devious daughter was there armed with new "comic rookie cards" which she made on her computer and passed around. Then she had the audience bring them up to me for autographs. I felt just like a celebrity, with lots of fans (but no pay). I did well, but some of my classmates were not so

## Col. Layton Park

lucky and died right there on the stage (comic talk for "got no laughs," which feels worse than dying).

The wife is great at coming up with these surprise gifts, but this time she may have created a monster because I discovered I love standing in front of people and making them laugh. Now I'm looking for new venues to present my routines in, and I speak for food.

If you are planning a surprise party, have me over. I'm a safe speaker to invite as I haven't yet died on stage and although I'm getting better with time, I still don't knock 'em dead either.

༄

- If Stupidity got us into this mess, then why can't it get us out?
- You can't say civilization isn't advancing; in every war they kill you in a new way.
- Always drink upstream from the herd.
- Never miss a good chance to shut up.
- It's not what you pay a man, but what he costs you that counts.

  Will Rogers- born: 1879-11-04 died: 1935-08-15

*A good surprise is having the Reno Star Riders, who I had never met before show up almost every day to offer support and take the wife to Supper.*

# 24. Hot Chocolate, Hot Women, Hot Vest

I had to go to Vancouver on Thursday for my daughter's wedding rehearsal. I didn't want to go and protested that I already know how to walk down the aisle, but the wife joined forces with the ex-wife to tell me if that were true, I wouldn't have had to make the trip twice.

So there I was, spending a warm spring day riding from Kelowna to Vancouver. Poor me. It took a full day of cruising as I decided to take my time and enjoy the road. An hour out of Kelowna and just past Penticton, I rode an extra five kilometers out of my way for ice cream cone in the sunshine at the world-famous Tickleberry's Ice Cream Store. While I was there, an old friend rode by with a herd of other automatic transmission Bergman scooter riders, known as the Shiftless Old Bastards (SOB's for short). He didn't even see me as they scooted by at high speed heading for the deserts of Osoyoos.

Then it was back to highway 3A, a winding ribbon of pavement leading to the quaint town of Keremeos. I passed the numerous fruit stands that silently stand guard along the way. Just out of Keremeos, I passed Asshole road (that really is the name, look it up on Mapquest), where I passed the fellow I'm sure it was named for.

The road continued thorough the Indian Reserve, winding along the Similkameen River to the almost ghost town of Hedley. Hedley is a must-stop. You look up and see hundred-year-old buildings hanging on the side of a high mountain cliff that once served the Mammoth gold mine.

Another few minutes down the road I stopped for a long, leisurely lunch in the town of Princeton. Continuing along, the Crowsnest became a true mountain road with signs saying "Curve – Slow to 30." Even on a bike, they don't mean 35. These curves are so sharp you have to be careful not to rear-end yourself.

As the road climbed higher, the air became cooler until ten-foot snow banks boxed in the sides of the highway and reflected the afternoon sun. I didn't stop at the beautiful Manning Park as I was now burning daylight and wanted to be out of the snow belt before sunset.

The highway joins the divided four-lane Trans-Canada Highway just outside the town of Hope, where I stopped for a well deserved hot chocolate

– then the final hour-long jaunt into Vancouver. This is truly a ride that everyone should have on their fifty-roads-to-ride list.

The wife drove down the following day in the motorhome and, looking gorgeous, accompanied me to our daughter's wedding. The bride was absolutely beautiful, and everything went flawlessly. It amazes me how much time brides spend planning every detail for this one special occasion, while the grooms strain just trying to remember which day it is and where to show up.

Sunday it was time to head for home, but rather than the long and winding road I traveled down on, I headed back the quickest way, the Coquihalla Highway. This four-lane road rises through several snow sheds to the top of the highest peaks, and then runs along the ridges to the interior of B.C. The connector, which leaves the highway at Merritt, crosses a range into the Okanagan.

This big wide highway, although filled with hills and curves, is made to dangle. If you ride at less than a buck-thirty, you are holding up traffic. The summit was lined with beautiful twelve-foot-high snow banks. The winds flowing down the passing mountain valleys across the snow convinced me to strap on the electric vest and turn on the heated grips.

I know, I know. Posers don't use this type of equipment, but real bikers who like to ride real mountain roads without shivering violently find it necessary, even on a cruiser. And if you make the trip in the shoulder season, don't leave home without them.

The warmth of the Okanagan flowed up the mountainside to meet me just outside Peachland, welcoming me home from a great weekend of hot chocolate, hot women and a hot electric vest.

*My BMW – Riding in the Snow*

# 25. The Community

The Star Chapter I belong to got a message that a chapter from Las Vegas was coming through town along with several riders from New York and we decided to do something to welcome them.

Some felt the justifiable thing to do to the Vegas crew would be finding someway to take all their money and send them home broke. Not that I ever came home from Vegas in that condition, but apparently some had. The New York riders presented a bigger problem. What could residents of Apple Valley show riders from the Big Apple?

We decided to invite the U.S. crew to attend a barbeque at our house, and finally I understood about community. With our crew, we had over fifty bikers bringing everything from salads and wonderful desserts to warmed-up road kill. (Don't tell anyone about the road kill, though. They thought it was casserole.)

Within minutes, the dozen members from the U.S. were like old friends. The Vegas crowd invited us to visit them and promised no gunplay. The New York group spoke Manhattan and I learned a few key common phrases in case I ever visit there, like "Step away from the gun" and "It's only a flesh wound."

The evening was outstanding. The wife's yuccaflats, a juice punch made from various fruit juices and ginger ale, mixed with the leftover dregs from our liquor cabinet and other secret ingredients, was more than partly responsible for warming up the community.

If you are planning a trip, contact members of your riding community in the various areas you will be passing through. I'm sure they will throw you an equally great welcome. If you are coming through our area, contact me as we still have some road kill left and it washes down good with yuccaflats.

The following day I decided to ride with the group as far as Merritt, and they asked me if I would lead. Of course, I was honored to, but it had been a while since I had ridden point. I was quickly reminded of what a demanding job that is.

*Col. Layton Park*

This was a great group that liked to ride in tight formation and by the rules. It's a pretty sight to look in your mirrors and see more than a dozen bikes winding behind, like the tail of a dragon.

I was watching them in my mirrors intently, only to discover they stop at yellow lights. Suddenly, the head was gone. It's embarrassing waiting beside the road for the followers so one can assume being the leader again. Something as simple as changing lanes can become difficult if you wish to keep the group together. It's sort of like driving the world's longest semi, only with more power and I was reminded of another issue: riding fast enough to keep the rocket men happy without leading the group into a speed trap.

Several from the group commented on the quality of the highway, saying they expected some sort of carriage road instead of an interstate sized road. They were surprised to find a highway that big considering there was no traffic on it. They enjoyed winding along the connector as it climbed out of the extremely hot Okanagan Valley, over the mountains where the air was so cold we had to stop and put on jackets, and then back down into the warmth of the beautiful Nicola Valley and Merritt.

In the end, it doesn't matter if you prefer heads or tale. Riding a dragon is always exciting, especially with your community.

☙

*A Motorcycle police officer in Cancun, Mexico, riding a Boulevard similar to my bike.*

# 26. Riding Alone in Cancun

"Sit down and have a beer." I turned to observe a tall thin man with graying hair and a fu Manchu moustache. "My name is Dave Rossman," he said in a deep Texan accent. "Can I help you?"

"Are these your bikes?" I said as I turned back toward five bikes setting in front of the small white stucco building with the open front and a covered patio, where the man was sitting.

"Yep. I have the coldest beer, ribs so good you will slap your mamma, and the best bikes to rent in Mexico.

"How much to rent a bike for a day?" I asked.

"Sit down and have a beer first," he said, so I pulled up a chair and joined him at a small table. It felt good to sit in the shade. He asked where I was from and what I rode. Then we talked about his bikes for a few minutes, and I said I was surprised he had only one Harley to rent.

He told me that besides the V-rod, he had a fat boy and a Heritage Soft Tail at home and one day he would be buried with one of them. "I am Harley to the bone. The boys back in Texas would laugh if they saw the other makes I have here." He went on to say the Hondas were the most popular and easiest to get parts and service for. "It's just good business to run them," he explained. "Besides, I put Cobra pipes on one and Vance and Hines on the other They may be Hondas, but they slobber real purdy."

We talked about what kind of riding I do and where the best places are to ride to from Cancun. He also asked about my four friends. The fellows were all about my age, owned similar businesses to mine and had years of experience riding a variety of bikes, so it should be good fun, I told him.

I later discovered his seemingly innocence questions were his way of his sorting out who he felt comfortable renting to. Apparently, my answers had passed.

"Give me American equipment, German Generals and Canadian soldiers, and I will rule the world!" said General Rommel, the Desert Fox, in 1944. That was the level of respect he had for Canadians. He admired their fury, their determination, and how fearless they were when facing the enemy. I am proud to be a Canadian and was certain my four Canadian friends were thoroughly capable of handling the challenges of a motorcycle ride in Mexico.

However, Rommel had another quote about Canadians: "If I could give every Canadian a bottle of whiskey and a motorcycle, I wouldn't have to kill them. They would kill themselves."

Some of the wives must have heard the second quote and feared that their husbands might get into the all-inclusive whiskey, because after I told them of Dave and the plan to go riding, the women stepped forward one by one and vetoed the trip.

I don't want to insinuate the proverbial young cat had whipped these four fellows, but suddenly the bravery of Canadian men seemed to be in question. "Yes, dear" was the expression of the day. "You promised no motorcycle riding in Mexico," hissed one man's wife. "It's just too dangerous." And that ended the conversation.

Was it scary at times? Yes, as scary as the King George Highway in Vancouver, the 401 in Toronto or the Deer foot in Calgary. And yes, your bike would be safer in the garage, but that is not what bikes are for.

Perhaps some riders should just buy a Sturgis tee-shirt at Wal-Mart, tie a dew rag over their neatly combed hair, invite friends over to the garage to sit and look at their bike while they tell them stories about how they almost took it out into traffic.

Just as I was about to give up when I met Lou, from Ontario, who said he rode a crotch rocket. I told him I was going for a ride down the coast in the morning, and he said he would love to come, so we arranged to meet in the lobby at 8 a.m. Then he turned to his wife, who was talking to some people, and told her about our plans. She gave him two thumbs up and smiled. Nice to know some women have faith in their men.

Lou and I had a great day riding along the ocean highway, stopping in small towns to eat at real seaside restaurants and touring local sites of interest.

We had a good last laugh when we got back to the hotel and found one of the "it's not safe in Mexico" motorcycle wives sitting in a wheel chair. It seems she slipped on the slick tiles at the resort buffet, fell and broke her foot. It just goes to show how dangerous Mexico can be.

*Accidents hurt - safety doesn't. Author Unknown*

# 27. Riding in the Rain

"If you don't ride in the rain, you don't ride." Dave said as we prepared to ride down the coast from Cancun to Playa De Carmen. A little tropical storm was not going to stop us as I have ridden in some of the worst storms in Western Canada, but this downpour was unbelievable. The water on the streets was already six inches deep.

"It rains hard here, but only for about five minuets," Texas Dave added in a slow drawl. "Have a beer, and we will wait." He was right. It rained hard for five minutes, which was followed by another five-minute rain, and then another five-minute one. The rain did let up in the early afternoon after a dozen beers but we wanted to ride a full day, sober, so we decided to book again for the following morning. In the meantime we enjoyed the ribs and watched as Dave saved the life of a young man and his wife from Toronto.

The man, in his early twenties, stood five-foot-six, weighed about a hundred-and-twenty-five pounds and asked to rent a big bike. His wife stood smiling beside him, several inches taller and seventy pounds heavier.

Dave peered over the top of the bottle and continued to suck on his beer for a moment, then asked the young man what he rode at home. The fellow smiled and said he didn't have a bike of his own.

"Where do you ride then?" Dave asked in his southern drawl.

"Well, mostly I ride quads in rural Ontario, but I'm pretty sure I could ride one of those." He pointed to Dave's big cruisers.

"Do you have a license?" Dave said.

"I have a general Ontario license that is good for bikes and cars."

"I'm afraid here you have to have a license that specifically says "motorcycle" on it."

"What about scooters then. Do you rent scooters?" said the young man.

"Nope, they're too dangerous. You don't want to be learnin' to ride a bike in crazy Cancun traffic, with a passenger who is obviously special to you." Dave smiled at the man's wife. "Best you get a specific license at home then come back and rent a substantial bike that drivers will hear and respect. I do have the coldest beer and best ribs in Cancun, though, if you'd like some."

"Thanks, but maybe we'll go shopping instead." Still smiling but looking somewhat dejected, the couple joined hands and walked away.

Dave looked at me and said, "I knew he wasn't a rider even before I asked him my four qualifying questions. I have never had anyone involved in an accident, and I want to keep it that way. It would be bad enough to have him try on his own, but with a passenger he wouldn't have made it two blocks. I'd feel just awful if someone came here on holidays then died on one of my bikes."

"You're right," I answered. "I can imagine the difficulty of having an inexperienced passenger, who considerably outweighed me, and I have a lot of years of riding. There must also be huge liabilities."

"Naw, not really. I pay a lot of insurance, and people can't sue like they do in the states. I just don't rent to anyone I think can't handle the bike." He took another sip of his beer. "Had a doctor and four friends show up once, all with licenses, and two struck me as good riders but the others were obviously new, so I turned 'em all down. That was a lot of money out of my pocket, but that's how it is here. I want everyone to have fun and go away recommending me to their friends. At the same time, I don't want to make anyone angry, because I want them to buy my beer and ribs."

I was still thinking about the young couple. "He didn't have a motorcycle license anyway, so you couldn't have rented to him if you wanted to," I remarked.

"Actually that's no big deal here. Most of the drivers don't have licenses. If there is an accident, the two parties work it out right there, and the one at fault pays. If they can't work it out and police think they're both at fault, then they each pay for the other's damage. If they can't work things out at all, then the police take them to jail until they do. It's pretty simple here. That's why I like it. I'm from Texas, so it has to be simple."

I looked at the vehicles rushing by and thought of the difficulty I had and foolish things I did when I was first learning to ride in a slower time with lots of open space. There is no doubt Dave saved that couple a lot of grief and probably their lives.

As the day wore on, a customer stopped by to tell Dave that a cop had pulled him over and charged him with speeding even though he was well under the speed limit. "He then told me the ticket would cost me a hundred-and-twenty-five dollars if he took me down to the police station, or I could just give him a hundred and he wouldn't give me a ticket. I didn't know what to do, so I gave him the hundred."

"He targeted you," said Dave. "Like it or not, both you guys look like gringos." He nodded toward me. "They know that white guys riding big bikes are probably not local. You should have just offered him ten dollars. That's probably all he really wanted anyway. You have to negotiate when you're in Mexico."

More folks joined us, some going upstairs to play pool, while two young women contemplated the sign that said, "Naked women get free beer" and asked if Dave would settle for just topless." I didn't stay to see how the negotiations ended.

☙

*Dave's two Hondas on a beach south of Cancun.*

**Leadership cannot just go along to get along. Leadership must meet the moral challenge of the day.**

– Jesse Jackson

Col. Layton Park

*Texas Dave in front of his pub.*

*Lou and I, with a young woman from Columbia,
Her husband wanted to take her photo with real bikers?*

# 28. Protective Wear

I earned my bike license in 1964, before there were helmet laws, and no, that does not explain my twisted view of life. I lived at the lake and rode daily in my cut-offs, tee shirts and thongs. Back then, "thongs" meant "flip-flops," not to be confused with the dental floss that doubles as bathing suit bottoms today.

But for the past several years, I have become a supporter of using protective clothing. I never ride the highways without my equipment: helmet, leather jacket, gauntlet gloves, leather chaps, protective eyewear and a head condom (dew rag). That was until the other day when the thermometer hit high marks and I was leaving a trail of sweat behind. It occurred to me in the forty-three years I have been riding, I have never had a serious accident. That suggests either that I am past due or that I ride with enough awareness that I am low-risk. Whatever the case, I shed most my gear and found new freedom again in riding the open road in only a tee shirt and sunburn.

I know the government means well and would like us all to get rid of the B.C. Beanie and wear helmets that run from the top of our heads to the soles of our feet. I wear a standard-issue half helmet, but I am thinking of joining the Sikh religion, the only people exempt from this law, so I can legally wear a padded dew rag.

Without protective gear, you could drop the bike at any moment and have to pick gravel from what is left of your skin. But you could also be hit by falling debris from the space station, or a bird with a rare and yet-undiscovered disease could fly through the office window and strike you, making you terminally ill.

The cousin of one of my friends was riding through a mountain pass when an elk lost its footing and slipped from a ridge above him, falling onto him and his bike. Had the elk been wearing protective apparel, perhaps they both could have been saved. Unfortunately, the elk died and the rider sustained brain injuries.

There are a lot of "could be's" out there. In the meantime more people are dying of heat exhaustion these days than from not wearing protective motorcycle gear. Of course, my research department consists of me making up eighty percent of the facts I use at the time of writing.

I read from a reliable source, that last year alone more people died walking alongside the road than in motorcycle accidents. It may be time to make pedestrians wear helmets.

"But you should not have a choice whether to wear a motorcycle helmet," the liberal left wing-nuts yell. "Who will pay the extra health care costs required to look after you if something happens?" Then they speed off in their Volvo without looking either way, cutting off two drivers as they go.

My youngest son recently commented on a news story about a family refusing to allow a blood transfusion for a dying loved one.

"I have no problem with that," he said, "It's all part of Darwin's natural selection process. From time to time, we need to thin the herd, and the dumb ones refusing medical help, or helmets, is one way to weed out the mentally weaker members."

Perhaps I fall into that category some days when I just can't stand to wear all the gear, but if it helps the herd, why shouldn't I have the right?

ぴ

I lean towards taking personal responsibility in my accident I had no broken skin because of my protective equipment even though I broke almost every bone on my left side.
Because of the rain I was wearing a full bell helmet yet I still suffered a concussion, I wonder how much worse I might have been had I been wearing my usual open face half helmet?
Sometimes leaders have to make unpopular decisions to set policy or rules for the good of all.

*Calvin Nelson and I an hour prior to the crash*

## 29. A Rolling Home Gathers No Moss

You have to be proud of a wife who loads up a thirty-three foot motor home, throws the son in, and heads out along on a 600-mile trip during one of the worst storms of the season.

Just because she is a woman and rides a scooter, a lot of men are amazed that she can handle a unit the size of a split-level home as capably as most fulltime truckers. The only trouble she has, according to the law, is keeping it under a buck and a half. But her charm and a, "I'm sorry Officer but could you just drag me out and beat me with your stick, I am in a bit of a hurry," followed by a great smile keep those tickets at bay. *(The editor felt I should remove this last line after all who would say that to a police officer? News flash... it has prevented 4 tickets as they just laugh and say they aren't allowed to do that anymore. Go ahead... try it but it must be with a smile.)*

Last week we met outside Edmonton and convoyed together to her family reunion at Granola Valley, home of all the fruits, flakes and nuts. She is a bit of an environmentalist, so she thinks it's great that between us we average over thirty miles per gallon. She at ten mile per gallon in the motorhome and me on the bike at fifty, which incidentally must be the I.Q. of the person who invented the trading of environmental credits, but let's not go there.

Her scooter, a Bergman, is capable of blowing half the cruisers off the road but on long trips, she is happier in the motorhome and I like its comforts. Does it sound wimpy for a biker not to sleep in the ditch beside the bike? It's just that I hate to be disturbed by mosquitoes making more noise than a two-cycle dirt bike race and large enough to carry away the tent. I'm getting long in the tooth and happy to put those days of super-rough behind me.

Now my idea of roughing it is getting only four or five channels on the TV as I lie on the couch drinking Okanagan wine at the end of a ride, and watching a rerun of *Easy Rider*. That movie never gets old, does it? Speaking of getting long in the tooth, it was good to see Fonda, if only for a nano-second, in *Wild Hawgs* as the ultimate biker.

Whether you're a rolling stone or have a rolling home, there is something special about sharing the road with others.

*Two-lane blacktop isn't a highway - it's an attitude.*

*Author Unknown*

*Col. Layton Park*

## Random Thoughts

**Not eBay Again?**
So a month after the accident I am laying around the house cruising ebay and wondering if I will ever ride again or what I should do next. I suddenly came across a 1938 Ford Hot Rod convertible with only 8 minutes left and no reserve! I hobble out the wife's office on the other end of the house to tell her about it but she has a client so without looking at it she shoos me away with the wave of her hand and says … "just do what ever the hell you want."

I don't know about you but I took this as permission to *do what ever the hell I wanted*? However she is a good sport and a month later, after she found a purple Mercedes Convertible that was *"just her color"*, we were talking again.

Okay, so I exaggerate a little. She loves both cars now, hers because it is real class, mine because it cost about the same as my bike and I tend not to fall off it. So now we enjoy taking turns cruising together through the Okanagan back roads. Wave if you see us.

*Layton and Myrna - 1938 "Pink Freud"*
*(Motorcycle replacement)*

# 30. I'd Rather Be Playing in Traffic!

"Golf is a good walk spoiled," according to Mark Twain, one of many things we agree on. In fact, I would be rather be playing in traffic than be on a golf course.

So when local Harley rider and manager of Qualico Homes, Guy Ouellette, called and asked if I wanted to spend the day sitting and watching golfers compete for a hole-in-one prize at the local builders' tournament, I said, "You've got to be kidding. I'd sooner watch them pound nails."

Then he added the magic words: "We have seats in the shade where we will be pounding back drinks."

It is hard work spending the day watching balls bounce everywhere but in the hole, while deciding on what the cart girl should pour next, but I was up to the task.

It was after two or six of these drinks that Guy saved my life. Not only did he save me, but he also saved you from a life-long inconvenience, as I am sure if it were not for his quick actions, the government would make it mandatory for bikers on golf courses to wear their helmets.

We were sitting back tipping a cold one when Guy said, "That one looks like it is headed straight for us."

"Huh?" I looked up, but couldn't see it. "Where?"

I was still scanning the sky for the little white globe when he jumped up from his chair. Leaping in front of me, Guy put his marshal arts training to work, batting the ball out of the air with the side of his gloved hand, just four feet short of my face.

The added padding of his leather-riding glove kept his hand from a serious owee and my face from one more divot.

So quick and unreal were his actions that only the golfers on the hole believed the story, with others saying it must be a fabrication brought on by a mixture of the hot sun and cold drinks. Even Guy's better half, Tina, not only didn't believe us – she took his gloves, saying he didn't need them on the course. But here it is, Tina, in black and white print, and everyone knows if it's in print, it has to be true. Thanks, Guy, but in the future, I think I'll keep playing in the traffic where it's less dangerous.

Col. Layton Park

Speaking of driving and traffic, I had an interesting encounter last week. I have a new book out on how to use self-hypnosis to remove those limiting roadblocks in your mind. The book is titled, "Get Out of Your Way." I was attending a book signing at the local Chapters store when a disheveled old man with wiry unkempt hair falling over a pair of coke-bottle-bottom glasses, stopped and looked at the title.

"Is that about driving trucks?" he mumbled as he picked up a copy. I thought he was kidding, so I said it was.

"Good," he said, "It's about time someone wrote a book about how to drive. I was coming in from Sicamous for those that have not driven that road, it is 80 k of two-lane, hilly highway that winds its way along the edge of a lake] and some truck driver rode right up close behind me and stayed there for miles. I find drivers often do that, and over the years, I've seen a number of accidents because they pull out and try to pass when it is unsafe to do so. You would think they would learn."

He put the book back down without discovering what it was really about, probably the same way he doesn't realize that on the road, it's he that is the problem. Watch for him, and ride safe while you are out there playing in traffic.

☙

*Layton and Guy sharing the story re-enactment may not be exactly the way the event occurred.*

## 31. e-Bay ... Bidder

My friend Bill Buterman buys cars on e-Bay then brings them into Canada and resells them for a profit. If he can do it, I can do it, I thought. What could possibly go wrong?

So for my first adventure I bid on a Mercedes wagon. I became excited and sent Bill an e-mail telling him I had the high bid for couple of days and the dead line was approaching.

"Looks like I may get this wagon... what do you think?"

His reply was short. "Nice car! Too bad you can't import it into Canada."

As I read his reply I could feel the adrenalin pump. How do I explain this to the wife, "Hey honey I bought us a great car but we have to leave it in the states. It will be handy to have something this nice to use when we visit there for a week or two every other year."

I know what some of you women are thinking, where did the wife find a resourceful guy like me. She is soooo... lucky.

"What do you mean I can't import this car?" I hollered at Bill when he picked up the phone.

He explained that I should have checked the government web site as to which cars are eligible for import and which are not. For some reason this particular model year is not.

My second lesson was that the serious buyers often do not bid until the dying seconds of the auction. Fortunately, that was the case this time. Someone outbid me at the last minute, and the conversation with the wife never had to take place.

That could be why it took me a couple of years and some research before I got up the nerve to do it again. Once I have a little knowledge on any subject I become an expert and some think dangerous. No sense bidding on cars anymore, I thought, so I moved up to motor homes.

My first successful bid turned out did not reach the reserve bid, and the owner would not return my messages so the bids were a waste of time.

On the next unit I was determined to buy, I sat on my final bid as the clock ticked down, then I hit the send button with only a second or two to go and presto, the auto bidding system topped my bid and I lost again. I learned that you could enter a maximum bid then let the auto system automatically up bid the next bidder immediately by a $100 until the bids reach your maximum.

I did not want to tip my hand on how much I was prepared to bid so I formed a new plan. I prepared my maximum bid but I did not hit send and waited for the dieing few seconds. With just ten seconds to go I hit the button, the wrong button and it took me right out of the web site. By the time I found my way back, the unit had sold for considerably less than my maximum bid. "Darn," I cursed.

Finally on the fifth unit I had it figured out and became the successful bidder on a 33', class A motor coach. It was mine, albeit it was located in Knoxville, Tennessee.

"That's great," I said to the wife, "We've never been to Tennessee, we can take our two sons and have an adventure!"

"It sounds like a great boy's get-a-way week," she said. "Why don't the three of you go?"

One week, ten states, 3,500 kilometers, two teenagers, it does sound like an adventure... I best get some help.

My friends just laughed at me then gave some lame excuse about having to seal the driveway that week.

I needed a childlike person who would get along with the three of us but was old enough to drive. Dave, my cousin's husband, immediately popped into my mind and he confirmed his qualifications by quickly agreeing.

"Wow, I am going to Tennessee to get my motorhome!" Will this be a fun adventure? On the other hand, will we find out why the motor home sold for so little? Will my friend Bill be impressed, or will there be some reason that the motorhome is un-importable?

One of the advantages of driving across the US in mid August is chances are high that you will end up in Sturgis during bike week. The adventure was almost a book by itself but ended successfully.

༄

*Riding a motorcycle on today's highways, you have to ride in a very defensive manner. You have to be a good rider and you have to have both hands and both feet on the controls at all times.*

- **Evel Knievel**

# 32. Jessie James, Outlaws & Bikers

We arrived about an hour before the original farm of Jessie James, in northeast of Kansas City, opened. Ignoring the "No Picnic" signs, we set up the barbeque and began making breakfast in the parking lot.

"I don't think we are allowed to do this," Liam said as concerned as a law abiding thirteen-year old can be.

"Liam, if we are going to do something illegal, what better place to do it than at the home of the world's most famous outlaw? I think Jessie would be proud of us." Dave responded with a smile. It is good to have another adult along to help teach moral issues to your children, I thought.

It was a great experience touring the old original farmhouse with the boys. They could understand the outhouse but could not believe that the young James boys had to live without a TV or refrigerator. "No wonder they turned to a life of crime." Carson said.

The James gang spent sixteen years criss-crossing the area robbing folks. It had taken us only three days crossing Tennessee, Kentucky, Illinois, and Missouri to discover the only outlaws left do not rob banks and trains, but now run tire stores and tow trucks.

We continued through Iowa and entered South Dakota noticing an ever-increasing number of motorcycles. Carson had now slept through six states, eight if you consider he never woke up in either Washington or Georgia as we drug him from one airplane to another.

We were beginning to think he was unconscious when a group of motorcycles went by and Dave remarked, "Look, those girls are all riding topless."

"Where?" Suddenly, Carson was alive and he sat up so fast he almost passed out from lack of blood to his brain.

"There!" said Dave pointing to the group, "How do they get away with that? Not one of them is wearing a helmet!" Carson groaned and flopped back onto the couch.

As we pulled into a rest stop for a break, easy rider followed us. I expected to see Peter Fonda as he removed his sunglasses and dismounted from a chopped Harley a perfect replica of the bike made famous in the movie.

*Col. Layton Park*

The fellow told us he was one of just five hundred thousand feared motorcycle hoods heading to Sturgis, South Dakota for the worlds largest motorcycle rally. Okay, so a dozen or so were feared gang members and the other half million were accountants, lawyers, doctors, and men of the cloth who shed their robes for a week to mount expensive motorcycles and ride like the wild bunch.

In Rapid City, the bikes crowded into service stations like flies on bad meat. There were so many bikes everywhere we could not find enough space to maneuverable the motor home in for gas. Fortunately, the coach carried enough fuel to travel over 500 miles, a fact that may be lost on the wife the first time she sees the price on the pump whirl past the purchase price of our last home.

Bikes or vehicles towing trailers holding bikes were now swarming around us as we headed to Mount Rushmore. The four stone presidents seemed to be looking down their noses in distaste at a parkade full of bikes. Motorcycles filled the mountain air with the constant rumble of engines. Grey haired people everywhere strode around in leather chaps, jackets adorned with crests and pins, and little do rags on their heads. It was refreshing to see people strut their individuality by all dressing the same.

Further, down the road we entered Deadwood, home to famous outlaws and lawmen such as Wild Bill Hickok, Wyatt Earp, Bat Masterson and Calamity Jane. The signs said "Motorcycle Parking Only" and bikes lined the streets for blocks. We parked on the outskirts then strode into town where the thunder of bikes was now so loud, that if Earp and Hickok had a shoot out no one would hear it.

Finally, escorted in to Sturgis, the motorcycle Mecca, we were now the center of one large mass of wheels, metal and noise that swept along the highway. Every James Dean wanna-be, every Marlon Brando worshiper, every Peter Fonda fan was here. Sturgis was crawling with Easy Riders, Rebels Without a Clue, or bikers just wetting themselves with the excitement of being here.

Jessie, Frank and the boys have long gone from the heartland, but the outlaw spirit is alive and well.

☙

"98% of all Harleys ever sold are still on the road. ...

              Harley Davision Advertisement

The other 2% made it home okay."        - Anonymous

# 33. Year of the Hog

2007 was the Year of the Pig... does that mean it was a bad year for receiving tickets... or was it really the Year of the Hog? A great year for Hog riders. I prefer to think of it as the second as I am looking forward to repeating the year in 2019. Seeing this prompted me to look for a horoscope for bikers and when I couldn't find one decided to just make one up.

For those born under these signs and born to ride the following is your official Biker horoscope.

**Aquarius (Jan.21 – Feb.18)** The Water Carrier is capable of becoming a long rider as you have the ability to carry your water the extra distance required and do not have to stand at the side of the road to drain it.

You are honest and loyal, Independent and intellectual but on the dark side you are perverse and unpredictable... unemotional and detached

If you were born under this sign you will find you have a long wait from the time you receive your birthday presents until riding season when you can actually use them. You will find little use for the new leather chaps for a while, unless you can convince the wife that is all she should wear around the house, which can help pass the long winter days.

**Pisces (Feb. 19 – March 20)** The Fishes ... you are imaginative and sensitive... intuitive and sympathetic but not so much you ride sidesaddle. On the dark side you are idealistic, secretive, and easily misled.

If this is your sign you have less time to wait until riding season but it is still too early to use that new beanie, unless you are a skier, then you can break it in on the hill.

**Aries (March 21 – April 20)** ... The Ram... you are enthusiastic, confident, dynamic and quick-witted. You also make a great long rider, as you really believe that old bike will get you there. On the dark side you tend to be foolhardy, a daredevil, impulsive and impatient wanting to ride earlier than good sense suggests.

The key is to maintain control and yes the roads look good but they can still have black ice early morning or late evening, unless you live north of Edmonton where they are still covered with three feet of that white stuff. It is time to tune your ride, as it will soon be time for the spring run-off.

*Col. Layton Park*

**Taurus (April 21 – May 21)** The Bull you are persistent and determined but on the dark side you can be jealous, possessive and inflexible about both your wife and your bike. You don't lend your ride to anyone, even to your best friend but don't understand why they shouldn't let you ride theirs. The bike I meant.

It is time to explore new boundaries as last years limitations are finally removed and this is the year to finally head for Sturgis.

**Gemini (May 22 – June 21)** the Twins both V and parallel…. Yes there are other motor styles out there. You are intellectual, eloquent and lively. On the dark side you tend to be nervous and tense.

Don't worry the May long weekend is a great time for the first long ride of the season.

**Cancer (June 22 – July 22)** The Crab … you are emotional intuitive and imaginative. On the dark side you are moody, overemotional and touchy.

Lighten up would you. I rode with you last year and I get tired of hearing how the rain is going to leave spots on your chrome.

Others may attempt to wrestle power away from you, but stand your ground. Your romantic and social sides will be busy if allowed the time out to play and explore. This summer may be a memorable one.

**Leo (July 23-Aug. 23)** The Lion… you are adaptable, warmhearted and faithful. You have been in this relationship for the past twenty-plus years and you have never strayed… you have never thought of mounting another… and Harley is thankful to you.

On the dark side you can be pompous, bossy and intolerant. Perhaps it is time you tried some strange stuff… take a test ride on a metric cruiser this year.

Morley said he read that a lion can make love a dozen times a day and he had to join Rotary instead.

**Virgo (August 24 – Sept. 22)** The Virgin… what they hell are you doing hanging out with this crew?

You tend to be modest and shy. You are practical, diligent, intelligent, and are driving the rest of us crazy.

On the dark side you can be fussy, a worrier, overcritical and harsh. It is time for you to join Taurus the bull and head for Sturgis where five hundred thousand bikers will try to change your sign for you.

**Libra (Sept 23. – Oct. 23)** The scales, my sign… we tend to be diplomatic, romantic and charming… Others see us as easygoing and idealistic. I didn't make that up… honest!

We don't acknowledge having a dark side but some may see us as indecisive, self-indulgent and gullible… proven by the fact that you have read this column this long and believe most of it is true.

*If You Are Going to Lead... Don't Spit!*

**Scorpio (Oct. 24-Nov.22)** The scorpion... you are forceful, passionate and determined to ride right up to the first snow.

On the dark side others may see you as compulsive, obsessive and obstinate. It is time to put your bike away for the winter...give it a rest.

**Sagittarius (Nov. 23- Dec 21.)** The archer-you are optimistic, freedom loving and philosophical. You think there is always one more good riding weekend left.

On the dark side you can be careless, irresponsible and that is the reason so many of the boys want to ride with you.

**Capricorn (Dec. 22 – Jan. 20)** the goat... and sometimes your beard even makes you look like one... you are practical, patient and humorous as you wait out the winter months wondering why the wife won't let you park your bike in the dinning room.

On the dark side you may become pessimistic, grudging and difficult to live with as the winter drags on. You just want to ride and your fantasies include quitting your job and moving to Mexico but the damn practical side won't let you.

*Col. Layton Park*

*If I'm out trailriding, I have a favorite motorcycle. Riding on the road, I've got a favorite. If I'm jumping, I have a favorite, and if I'm racing, I have a favorite.*
— **Evel Knievel**

*Vegas Police Officer at Bike Fest filling Nevada in on my map patch.*

*Life may begin at 30, but it doesn't get real interesting until about 150.*
*Author Unknown*

# About the Author

**Layton Park - C.Ht. CPBA, CPVA, RET**

Layton is a partner in several service-focused businesses and consults to companies wanting to improve their performance in the area of communication, goal setting, sales and profitability.

Layton is also a keynote speaker and expert in the following topics.
1. Leadership
2. Mental Toughness
3. Goal Setting
4. Strategic planning
5. Succession planning
6. Humor in the workplace
7. Communication
8. Team building
9. Power of Hypnotic Suggestion

For additional topics or custom talks contact
info@max-u.com
Info@GPS 4 Biz.c om

# Books by Layton Park

| | |
|---|---|
| | **Get Out of Your Way** |
| | **Unlocking the Power of Your Mind to Get What You Want** |
| | or - How to Remove Limiting Beliefs Through the Power of Self-Hypnosis |
| | Discover what beliefs or fears are holding you back, how you can change them and succeed in your goals. |
| | Trade Paperback 9780738710525 |
| | 6 x 9 - 216 pages Published March 2007 by **Llewellyn** - New Worlds of Body, Mind & Spirit |
| | **Spirit Doctor** |
| | *The Hypnotic Healing Practice of Phineas Parkhurst Quimby* (Dr. Park 1802 – 1866) |
| | This is the story of America's most influential hypnotist, spiritual mind, and Father of New Thought. |
| | A man responsible for numerous healings using practices and methods scientifically explained by Dr. Bruce Lipton in his book, The Biology of Belief. |
| | Published by: iUniverse |
| | ISBN 978-0-9732111-3-9 |
| | 6 x 9 – 109 pages Published 2010 |

**Trade Secrets**

Layton Park and Myrna Park

*The secret of managing relationships at home and work*

This compelling business parable is about a tradesman who, together with his wife, builds a very successful business. That is until the day the three division managers tell him he has to make a choice between them and keeping his wife involved in the business.

Published by iUniverse
ISBN 978-0-9732111-2-2
6 x 9 – 120 page - 2010

**If You Are Going To Lead ... Don't Spit!**

This book is a collection of motorcycle stories from Layton's humour columns in the Busted Knuckle Chronicles. The lessons in leadership in each story remind us that leaders are everywhere and instrumental in everything we do.

Published by iUniverse
ISBN 978-0-9732111-5-3
6 x 9 – 81 page - 2010

## Chicken Coop...
##                for a Rubber Sole

This book is collection of stories from Layton's columns in North of Fifty. These humorous stories are great short reads, ideal for airports or traveling where you may want to enjoy something light and fun. This book is an ideal inexpensive gift that can be easily re-gifted and enjoyed by people of all ages.

Published by iUniverse
ISBN 978-0-9732111-6-0

### Don't Drink the Kool-Aid
*How big business, government and religion use hypnotic techniques to influence their followers.*

This book, scheduled for release Winter 2011 is a "must- read", for anyone wanting to position their organization in the minds of their customers and employees or wanting to understand how other big institutions are doing so to them. Advance orders are available from the publisher in quantities of 20 for only $200 plus shipping.

Contact info@max-u.com